THE DUCHESS

STANIER'S MASTERPIECE

The inspiration of the 'Duchess' and the catalyst for all the significant engineering changes at the LMSR, Sir William A. Stanier FRS, seen here in an official photograph dated 1938.

National Railway Museum, York

THE DUCHESS
STANIER'S MASTERPIECE

ROGER J. MANNION

ALAN SUTTON PUBLISHING LIMITED

First published in the United Kingdom in 1996
Alan Sutton Publishing Ltd · Phoenix Mill · Far Thrupp · Stroud
Gloucestershire

British Library Cataloguing in Publication Data

A catalogue record of this book is available from the British Library

ISBN 0-7509-0903-X

Typeset in 10/13 pt Sabon.
Typesetting and origination by
Alan Sutton Publishing Limited.
Printed and bound in Great Britain by
Butler & Tanner Ltd, Frome and London.

CONTENTS

A 'Duchess' at Paddington. No. 46229 *Duchess of Hamilton* at Paddington's platform one on 4 November 1994, in BR red livery. No. 46229 had travelled up from the Didcot Railway Centre to publicize the 'Shakespearian' service on the following day.

Author's Collection

PREFACE AND ACKNOWLEDGEMENTS

A lot has been written about the 'Princess Coronation Pacific' class over the years, some critical but most in praise of Stanier and his team's achievements. That the class was handsome, I think goes without saying, particularly those members which were not originally streamlined. Notwithstanding, the streamlined 'Duchesses' were attractive in the context of their time and certainly achieved a great deal of good publicity, and bonding, as the modern business managers would say, within the LMS. Contrary to some modern critiques of the class, I believe that the 'Duchesses' did help finally to pull together the differing parts of the London Midland and Scottish Railway under one banner.

All engineering designs are the unique results of human endeavour and how the instigators of those designs are able to express themselves within the parameters that affect them at the time. It was Stanier's skill in taking and developing a mix of disparate ideas from the different companies within the LMS which was instrumental in producing a classic locomotive design. I have tried to put together some of these human influences in an attempt to show how the design was built up of compromises and the interaction of differing views. I also hope that I have been able to describe the engineering achievements and performances so that the power, quality and vitality of the 'Duchess' class of locomotive can be appreciated.

My first memory of a 'Duchess' was as a young train spotter sitting on the wooden fence alongside the West Coast Main Line at King's Langley between the signal-box and the station, when one of the older boys shouted, 'It's a "Duchess".' To this day I have no idea which one it was other than to remember this slightly scruffy, very big, red locomotive go speeding by with the characteristic four-cylinder beat.

The quadruple track at this point was towards the end of a long straight and was renowned for high speeds on the non-stop main-line services. It was not uncommon for the 'Midday Scot' and other named expresses to exceed 90 m.p.h. on this stretch. In those days it was possible to sit close to the line and hear the signal bells from the signal-box and see the signals being pulled, unlike today with the massive concrete M25 flyover passing right across where we used to sit.

We would cycle to the Gypsy Lane portal entrance to the Watford tunnel, which consisted of two bores. We always watched the fast lines and were extremely disappointed when we saw in the distance a semi-fast fitted goods hauled by a 'Duchess' disappearing into the cutting of the 'slow' tunnel. In the late fifties, the autumn of steam traction on British Railways, it was still possible to see the full range of both new and pre-nationalization motive power – 'Britannias', Deltic diesels (some in original manufacturers' colours), and of course the 'Duchesses'. I suppose we were lucky in that we didn't have to travel all over the country to see the complete range of LMS motive power and also had a shed nearby at Watford to 'cop' the branch-line and local passenger services locomotives.

I have tried to reproduce different views of the 'Duchess' class to those that have been published before, and I have also included some photographs and logs that have never been published before. At the same time I have attempted to bring together as much information as possible so that the enthusiast has a single source for details of the 'Duchesses'. I appreciate that some of this information has been published previously but I have taken the opportunity of cross-checking some of the details in an attempt to verify any discrepancies. I hope I have been successful, but while sources and references have been checked in great detail I would freely admit that any errors are totally mine and not the responsibility of the contributors. I would also admit to having a bias towards the 'Duchesses' but have tried to keep it in check and not to let it colour my engineering judgment.

One of the pleasant things about producing a work of this kind is that not only do you learn a great deal of new information about a subject you enjoy but also you meet new friends and renew old acquaintances along the way. I would therefore like to thank the following people for their help and support: John Wickham for his time, photographs and logs, and especially his advice and anecdotal information; Ray Towell and Phil Atkins at the National Railway Museum for help and assistance in my research; Dr Jim Andrew at the Birmingham Museum of Science and Industry for the photograph, and technical information and assistance; and Jonathan Wheeler and James Hutchenson at the Bressingham Steam Museum and Gardens for their hospitality and kindness, and for allowing me to crawl all over *Duchess of Sutherland*. All National Railway Museum photographs are provided courtesy of the Science & Society Picture Library, London. Finally, I would also like to thank two good friends who assisted with editing and copy facilities – 'Buster' Dodson and Peter Hall.

The final word must go to the footplate crew from Willesden shed who described the 'Duchesses' in the late fifties as the 'Rolls-Royce' of locomotives.

R.J. Mannion
February, 1996

A DUCHESS AT PADDINGTON

Climb the stairs of the Circle Line exit to Paddington main-line station and you are greeted by the vista of Brunel's magnificent London terminus, filled with rush-hour travellers scurrying to the office or the City. Struggling to cross this human stream you find yourself suddenly confronted with the *Duchess of Hamilton*, quietly simmering alongside platform one, in its BR crimson livery and with gleaming, oily rods. You could have been transported back to the locomotive exchanges of 1948, but then alongside the 'Duchess' appears a modern WR diesel-powered HST, and it is back to the reality of 1994!

The *Duchess of Hamilton* had been brought up from the Didcot Railway Centre to publicize the steam-hauled trips to Stratford-upon-Avon and Bristol that weekend, having the previous day been positioned from York. The commuter and InterCity trains continued to arrive and it was interesting to note the reaction of the morning passengers as they wended their way towards another day of stress and strife. As they passed the proud and haughty 'Duchess', otherwise stiff upper-lipped businessmen broke into animated conversation, ladies who pretended not to be interested in trains displayed hints of smiles at some half-forgotten memory, and children too young to know steam power were fascinated by big engineering in a world of miniaturization. If nothing else, the 'Duchess' had a very positive effect on those people, leaving them with a memory to cherish and a completely different topic of conversation for the day ahead.

Surprisingly, some people questioned the footplate crew on whether this was the train to Bristol or Newbury or some other destination on Network Southeast, and it seemed that steam traction was totally irrelevant to them! Even more amazing was the enquiry from one young man who asked why there was a diesel at the front of the engine, mistaking the smoke from the chimney for a diesel exhaust. It took some time to convince him that the smoke was coal-derived and the engine was a genuine steam locomotive!

The footplate crew consisted of a Southern Region driver, a Great Western Region fireman and a Great Western inspector, crewing a LMS Pacific locomotive. Ribald comments were rife about the comparative attributes of the 'Castles' and 'Kings', or the Bulleid Pacifics against the 'Duchess'; the ease of firing of the wide Belpair firebox, or right- or left-hand drive; it was all good friendly rivalry but underneath lay a genuine love of steam traction. This banter truly indicated the

The old and the new. *Duchess of Hamilton* at Paddington on 4 November 1994 alongside
a Western Region HST.

Author's Collection

evocative nature of steam on an otherwise bleak Friday morning, particularly
considering that the crew had loaded 6 tons of coal the night before, by hand!

The morning left a lingering memory of the sounds and smells of a previous age
which was probably dirty, inefficient and sometimes downright archaic, but yet
for all that, the emotive and nostalgic themes of childhood persisted. A good
memory and a good day.

CHAPTER ONE

A BACKGROUND TO THE TIMES

Steam locomotives were the result of human imagination, endeavour, thought and labour, where human frailties and differences were exhibited in the solutions to specific engineering problems. Problems resulted from, among many other things, financial pressures, passenger loadings and route profiles – so that the footplate crews and locomotive designers who solved these problems became household names. In the steam era didn't all young boys want to be engine drivers?

There was something very special about the railways, fostered and encouraged, no doubt, by the main railway companies. Major intercompany rivalries both pre- and post-Grouping led to significant differences between the post-Grouping operating companies. This could be seen in every facet of the companies' operations, including signalling, stations, and coaches and locomotive design. The largest company was the London, Midland and Scottish Railway, which at the time of the Grouping in 1923 had 9,179 locomotives from nine different railway companies, who in turn had different operating requirements and designs. From this mix of different cultures were born, arguably, the pinnacle of British steam locomotive design, the 'Duchesses'.

The LMS 'Princess Coronation Pacific' class of locomotives – the 'Duchesses' – were considered the most handsome and aesthetically pleasing engines built for a British railway, Gresley A4 and GWR passenger engines notwithstanding. That they were successful and efficient, both from the passengers' and the footplate and service crews' points of view, only adds to the greatness of this class of locomotive.

To understand why the class evolved in the way it did, one has to explore a little of the background of the times under which it was designed and to understand the influences that shaped the genius of the man who conceived the design – William, later Sir William, A. Stanier.

Stanier was born in Swindon on 27 May 1876. His father was the chief clerk to William Dean of the Great Western Railway, so consequently it was not surprising that Stanier was to take an apprenticeship with the GWR in May 1892. He had been an office boy with the company since January of that year, being too young previously to start his apprenticeship. Interestingly enough, in June 1876 Nigel Gresley was born to a Derbyshire clergyman, just one month after Stanier's birthday. Almost from the beginning, the lives of these two great railway engineers were to become entwined.

At the very start of Stanier's apprenticeship the GWR was undergoing momentous culture changes. Over one weekend in May 1892 the final broad gauge GWR lines were converted to standard gauge, and it is probable that these changes helped teach Stanier the flexibility which enabled him to pull together the disparate cultures of the London Midland and Scottish Railway when he eventually became Chief Mechanical Engineer.

Having completed his apprenticeship, Stanier held a number of posts within the GWR over the next thirty years, including working in the drawing offices, as Locomotive Mechanical Inspector, Divisional Locomotive Superintendent, Assistant Works Manager and then Works Manager, all at Swindon. Finally, he became Principal Assistant to C.B. Collett. Stanier worked for three different CMEs during his time, the most notable of which was George Jackson Churchward, of whom Gresley stated, at a meeting of the Institute of Locomotive Engineers in 1936, 'I have always thought, and still think, that locomotive

No. 6224 *Princess Alexandra* in immaculate condition, taking water at Shrewsbury in 1938 during a running-in turn.

National Railway Museum, York

engineers in this country owe more to the ingenuity, inventiveness and foresight of Churchward than to any other Chief Mechanical Engineer.' Little wonder that the Swindon influence was to be so apparent in the designs of the LMS.

The late twenties and early thirties were a bad time for Britain and the rest of the world, with a severe and general trade depression, major industries suffering a lack of orders and the demand for coal substantially reduced. These difficulties produced a recession in rail freight traffic and of course reduced passenger receipts. Against this background the board of the LMS was struggling to overcome once and for all the problems caused by the merger of a number of historically and culturally different companies, all with individual designs, CMEs and company philosophies.

It was as part of these changes that Stanier was invited by Sir Josiah Stamp, then President of the Executive, to become the Chief Mechanical Engineer of the LMS. Stanier was appointed on 1 January 1932. It is probably true to say that Stanier was charged with solving the chaotic engineering problems that then existed on the LMS. The fact that he succeeded is only too obvious from his legacy.

One of the main areas that concentrated the minds of the board of the LMS was the rivalry between the east and west coast routes to the North. This rivalry went back to the days of the Midland Railway's new route to the North, when it reduced fares and decreased journey times, thus giving the travelling public a real choice. The route competition has continued periodically ever since and was increasingly prevalent during Stanier's tenure of the LMS in the thirties. This was particularly as a result of the advent of Gresley's streamlined A4 Pacifics built for the LNER's east coast route.

Clearly the success of any service can only be assured if it provides the customers with what they require. As Britain came out of recession, a desire grew for travelling in more luxury and comfort, with more convenience and at greater speeds. Already the aeroplane was seen as a possible competitor for long-distance travel and road transport was beginning to take freight and some passenger traffic away from the railways. To survive, both the LMS and the LNER had to compete. The LNER's success on its North of England and Scottish services spurred the LMS to increase speeds on the west coast routes and ultimately to design powerful new locomotives for the services.

As the depression ended, the desire to do away with the cheerless, grey, deprivation resulted in striking new designs full of vitality and colour, even a certain frivolity. This need to forget encouraged designers to produce a wide variety of different and sometimes aesthetically pleasing designs. This was all part of a general feeling of confidence slowly returning to the nation.

Increased competition on the east and west coast main lines forced the LMS and the LNER to offer far better services both in terms of faster trains and better on-board conditions. This led to the special trains particularly to Scotland, and in turn meant that new engines were required. Gresley was first to produce a

The first three brand-new streamlined 'Coronation' class Pacifics outside Crewe paint
shops on 18 June 1937. From the front, No. 6220 *Coronation*, No. 6221 *Queen Elizabeth*
and No. 6222 *Queen Mary*.

National Railway Museum, York

spectacular engine for the LNER's route, and in fact the A4s had been operating
on the East Coast Main Line for almost two years before the LMS introduced its
new design.

The Bugatti-inspired A4 design was part of the growing confidence and belief in
Britain at the time. Certainly the publicity generated by the services operated by
the A4 engines had a major impact on the whole approach to long-distance rail
travel, and one can also argue, from an engineering point of view, that the value
of the streamlined A4, its public appeal and influence on other services and
railway companies were considerable. Thus from this melting pot of
intercompany rivalry and national change was born the 'Princess Coronation' or
'Duchess' class of Pacifics.

Pacific locomotives were, until the thirties, an unusual sight on British metals.
Even though the arrangement had originated in the USA as early as 1886, and
despite the clear advantages in its use on fast passenger locomotives, the 'Princess
Royal' Pacifics were not introduced on LMS metals until after 1933 and even then
were considered innovative. Up to 1933 only three classes of Pacifics existed in
Britain, and two of those had passed into oblivion in a very short time.

In 1908 the GWR had put into service *The Great Bear*, numbered 111. It was designed by G.J. Churchward and was the earliest British Pacific, but as it was the only member of its class, it consequently had a limited influence on future designs. When the inner firebox needed renewing in 1923 it was decided to rebuild the locomotive as a 'Castle'. Thus *The Great Bear* was withdrawn from service on 7 January 1923 and ultimately was outshopped as 'Castle' class No. 111 *Viscount Churchill*.

Sir Vincent Raven designed a Pacific for the NER and they were put into service in November 1922. Eventually they became LNER class A2, but were to be withdrawn in 1936–7.

At the time Stanier became CME of the LMS, the LNER was operating a number of Gresley Pacific designs which ultimately led to the design and construction of the A4 class. It was the success of the A4s, coupled with the results of using Stanier's 'Princess Royal' class on the West Coast Main Line, which concentrated the minds of the LMS Board. The 'Princess Royal' Pacifics had been used by the LMS with great success, but for the Scottish runs it was acknowledged that, with the higher speeds and longer distances involved, a locomotive with a capacity for sustained high-speed steaming was required. The LMS Board agreed that new locomotives should be built during 1937, the coronation year of King George VI and Queen Elizabeth, and that they would be known as the 'Princess Coronation' class, or 'Duchesses' as they were ultimately known.

From a brief examination of the route profile for the Euston–Carlisle main line and on into Scotland, it can be seen that a need existed for very powerful and efficient locomotives; at one point, on the rise to Shap Summit, there are nearly 4 miles at a gradient of 1 in 75. This presents little difficulty for modern electric- or diesel-powered locomotives but in the days of steam, banking and, in some cases, double-heading were the order of the day. Previously, because of the smaller locomotives available for the route, loads and speeds were restricted even when using banking engines and double-headed trains, and while the pride and skills of both footplate crews and shedmasters produced excellent timings, the wear and tear on locomotives and crews was beginning to have a significant effect on service provision. Clearly, with the need to meet the competition from the LNER and to recoup the loss of revenue due to that competition, the LMS needed larger trains with more luxurious stock. This meant heavier trains, which had to maintain faster timings over the whole route, which in turn meant there was a requirement for larger and more powerful locomotives.

The 'Princess Coronation' class was Stanier's last new design and the locomotives remained fundamentally unchanged throughout their working lives. Certain peripheral changes were made, including the ultimate removal of the streamlined casing, but the locomotives required little modification due to service or design faults. The 'Duchesses' were designed by a team of engineers blessed with great skills and talent, led by a CME who was at the height of his powers.

No. 46225 *Duchess of Gloucester* waits to take the Glasgow to Liverpool relief forward from Carlisle on 26 March 1964. The relief has just arrived on the left behind 'Black Five' No. 45013 and 'Jubilee' No. 45635 *Tobago*; note the dieselization to the right of the 'Duchess'.

John Wickham

The 'Duchesses' gave exemplary service for twenty-seven years, and during that time produced some exceptional performances, one in particular regarding the *Duchess of Gloucester*, No. 46225. She pounded up the 1 in 100 to Ais Gill with a 420 ton train, which included a mobile test unit, at 30 m.p.h. The test unit was working against the locomotive to give an equivalent load of 900 tons. The sight and sound of that exploit must have been magnificent.

Part of the success of the 'Duchesses' was their superb steaming ability with a total evaporative heating surface of 2,807 sq. ft and the ease with which the footplate crew could fire the boiler via the very large grate. O.S. Nock, in his book *A History of the LMS*, relates how he had first-hand knowledge of the ease of firing these massive engines: '. . . the coal was gently fed through the door and it appeared to distribute itself ideally over the grate'. Whether the firemen felt the same is arguable but Stanier and his team had certainly gone to great lengths to make sure that the steaming qualities matched all the demands required of the locomotive, with a large boiler containing one of the biggest superheaters in a British locomotive – at forty elements and 856 sq. ft, (ultimately reduced to 830 sq. ft) – and a large grate area of 50 sq. ft. In addition, Stanier took full advantage

No. 46235 *City of Birmingham* and No. 46245 *City of London* at Willesden shed on 26 January 1964. No. 46235 seems to be taking water.

John Wickham

of the advances in internal streamlining for steam passages, initially put forward by the French engineer André Chapelon. Particular attention was paid to the front-end design so that the freest passage of steam could travel via the cylinders. The result was a free-steaming locomotive which more than fulfilled the demands of long and sustained steaming, particularly over the West Coast Main Line.

A further innovation which Stanier brought to locomotive design was the standardization of the cab design and a consideration for the footplate crew's comfort. Nevertheless, compared with the air-conditioned, electronic comfort of today's HST crews, steam footplatemen had an arduous and tough task. Maybe it was partly because of this consideration that the crews showed great loyalty to the class. Certainly the fact that the locomotives were good steamers and were fitted with a coal-pusher from the start had something to do with it, but the top-link crews, particularly from Camden, who were allocated to the 'Duchesses' were extremely loyal, not only to the class but in some cases to a particular locomotive.

The first five 'Duchess' class locomotives were built in streamlined form in 1937, as were the second batch of five, built in 1938, but there seemed to be divergence of purpose among the design team over the advantages of the streamlining, as the next batch of five, also built in 1938, were non-streamlined. The next fourteen, built between 1939 and 1943, were again streamlined, while

City of Sheffield, No. 6249, seen here at Crewe on 21 September 1944. She was the first nonstreamlined member of the second batch built and is shown in wartime black livery complete with a streamlined tender. *City of Sheffield* was fitted with a stainless steel name-plate on 1 November 1944.

National Railway Museum, York

the final nine were built in nonstreamlined form between 1944 and 1948. All the locomotives were built at Crewe locomotive works.

Extensive work had been carried out to produce the final streamlined design, though the effects of the additional weight of streamlining on the performance of the locomotive have never been comprehensively investigated. Most experts are of the opinion that there was little or no improvement in performance, but the locomotives and the trains they hauled were a public relations man's dream and gave the LMS the publicity boost it very much needed at that time.

A few days before the inauguration of the public service of the 'Coronation Scot', which took place on 29 June 1937, a demonstration run was made, which coincidentally occurred the day before a similar trip made by the LNER. Much has been written about this trip, and the 'successful' attempt on the British speed record for rail travel. There are undoubtedly some discrepancies regarding the actual speed attained, and also some safety implications because of the risks taken on the approach to Crewe. The description 'successful' is highlighted because even though Stanier's personal assistant, Riddles, was on the footplate as an observer during the journey and the engine speed recorder chart showed a speed of 114 m.p.h., O.S. Nock and the late Cecil J. Allen were also present as observers on the journey and recorded an agreed peak of 113 m.p.h. The discrepancy in recording the maximum speed, coupled with the near catastrophic high-speed negotiation of the three successive crossovers on the approach to Crewe, are indicative of the

Sir William A. Stanier FRS on the through line at Carlisle, heading south on 20 August 1956, passing an unknown 'Duchess' on the Up platform in the background. Note the electric headlights.

National Railway Museum, York

pressures both the LMS and LNER were under at that time. It is worth noting that the coaches gave a near disastrous ride during the approach to Crewe but the locomotive coped admirably with the ill treatment.

During the Second World War, in common with all British locomotives, the 'Duchess' class gradually lost the colourful liveries of the thirties and, as they were out-shopped from repair or rebuild, they appeared in uniform black, which became more and more shabby with time. In addition, the disruptions of war, with the Blitz and the need for men to join the forces, meant that the railway system in general became more run down. Locomotives were given less maintenance, the permanent way was allowed to deteriorate, and sheds and footplates were manned by less well-trained staff. For all that, the 'Duchess' worked well and hard with exceptional loads, sometimes in excess of twenty-two coaches. Apart from the addition of smoke deflectors as a result of the accident at Ecclefechan in 1945 (see p. 107), no major changes were made to the design throughout this difficult period.

After the war, there were further improvements and H.G. Ivatt, who was to become the final CME for the LMS in January 1946, added roller bearings, a rocking grate, self-emptying ashpan and self-cleaning smokebox. While these additions improved the maintenance and availability of the class, they did not impinge on the original concept of Stanier, a great credit to the design of the locomotives and the team that designed and built them.

The locomotives lasted well into the autumn of steam, and although in later years they were not allowed south of Crewe because of the overhead catenary, they performed sterling work on the routes to the North. Sadly, most were used on freight traffic, although *Sir William A. Stanier FRS*, No. 46256, continued to provide the motive power for excursion trains some time after the rest of the class was withdrawn in September 1964.

A relation of the 'Duchesses' was the Turbomotive, No. 46202, which, when built in 1935, was unnamed. She was not a 'Coronation' class at all, and started life as a heavily modified 'Princess Royal' class, fitted with turbine drive rather than pistons. Subsequently, when the cost of completely replacing the turbines became uneconomic, she was rebuilt with standard piston drive and named *Princess Anne*. The rebuild was based on the front end of the 'Duchess' class and consequently from the front there was a very striking resemblance between the two designs. Unhappily, *Princess Anne* was involved in the 1952 Harrow and Wealdstone disaster, and was damaged beyond economical repair. She had only completed 11,443 miles since being rebuilt. The accident also involved another of Stanier's Pacifics, No. 46242 *City of Glasgow*. This locomotive was rebuilt after the accident and was not withdrawn until 1963.

The complete story of the 'Duchess' Pacifics is one of human endeavour, and of a hunger for success and engineering excellence, exhibited in the beauty and grace of a steam leviathan which remained in the same basic form for over twenty-seven years, providing both the public and the railway companies with performance and service that had never been previously attained.

It is interesting to note that Stanier produced drawings in 1942 for a passenger express locomotive using the 4–6–4 wheel arrangement, but still based solidly on the 'Duchess' class design, even down to replicating the streamlining. Further, the soundness of the design is exemplified by the continuation of the design practices of the 'Coronation Pacifics' on the large standard BR classes of locomotive, in particular the 'Britannias'.

Thus it was that on 5 July 1937 the first passenger-carrying 'Coronation Scot' was inaugurated between London and Glasgow, powered by a great locomotive which had been created by a team of excellent designers inspired and motivated by a superb engineer and leader.

CHAPTER TWO

NEEDS AND EVOLUTION

The period prior to Stanier's appointment as Chief Mechanical Engineer (during 1923 to 1932) had been a time of much discord between the CME and operating departments of the LMS – so much so that ten years after the Grouping in 1923 the LMS still did not have the motive power capability to operate over the complete West Coast Main Line between London and Glasgow. The line was the company's premier route, competing directly against the LNER on the east coast, where the Gresley Pacifics were already making a real impact.

Before 1932 the speeds and timings of the London to Scotland express services were restricted by the long-standing agreements made after the 'Races to the North' of 1888 and 1896. This meant that services were not allowed to cover the distance in less than 8¼ hours, so to some extent there was no incentive for the LMS to build larger, more powerful engines. The LMS express services to the North changed engines at Carnforth, typically using LNWR 4–6–0 Claughtons from London and then double-heading Midland 4–4–0 Compounds from Carnforth to the North. Clearly, this was an unsatisfactory state of affairs. The unhappy situation was further complicated by the need for more power on the massive East Midlands to London coal trains which were inevitably double-headed and moved very slowly through the Home Counties.

While the problems were recognized, they could only be solved by the people running the departments to which the problems related. As always, it was the personalities and their own prejudices which influenced the outcome. At the time of the Grouping, George Hughes, ex-CME for the combined LNWR and Lancashire and Yorkshire railway, was appointed CME for the LMS, in preference to Sir Henry Fowler, who became his Number Two. Fowler had been CME for the Midland Railway, and J.E. Anderson, who became responsible for the operational affairs on the LMS, was also from the Midland. It was therefore not surprising that the influence of the Midland had an impact on Hughes' thinking, and consequently Midland practices were almost bound to be perpetuated. The Midland Railway, with its small and frequent lightweight trains, hauled by the Derby designs with typically short-travel valve gear and undersized bearings, thereby influenced the whole of LMS thinking and inevitably held back the development of new and more powerful locomotive designs.

Queen Elizabeth at Glasgow Central in 1937, on what seems to be a local train. Note the single lamp on the chimney. Certainly the streamlined locomotive is attracting a lot of attention from passengers and commuters.

National Railway Museum, York

Both Hughes and Fowler, who was to follow Hughes as CME, developed designs for a Pacific class of locomotive, but these efforts were thwarted by the Midland Railway bias of the operating department. In particular, Fowler's Compound Pacific design was frustrated by the operating department's use of a loaned GWR 'Castle' class locomotive and its use for revenue-earning traffic between London and Crewe. It is understood that Fowler was not aware of this decision prior to the event – obviously power struggles and politicking are not just modern phenomena. The only positive aspect of the cancellation of the Fowler Pacific project was the design and construction of the 'Royal Scot' 4–6–0 class, the order for fifty locomotives being placed with the North British Locomotive Company in January 1927, with completion on 15 November the same year.

Hughes' design for a Pacific class was a result of the need for a powerful goods locomotive to haul the heavy coal trains from the Midlands to London. As part of this requirement, his design for the coal train locomotive was for a 2–8–2 which met the axle load limitations set by the civil engineer. At the same time, in an attempt to standardize designs, a 4–6–2 design with similar constituent parts was

No. 46245 *City of London* over the pits at Willesden shed on 26 January 1964. Note her immaculate condition, in BR red livery.

John Wickham

put forward for the West Coast Main Line services. Interestingly, this design was to have four cylinders and an eight-wheel tender to carry up to 8 tons of coal, as opposed to the normal $5\frac{1}{2}$ tons of the standard Derby tender. Again, this design was frustrated by the operating department.

Hughes was originally a CME on the LNWR, which had its own mechanical engineering centre at Horwich. Hughes decided to keep this as the centre of excellence for the LMS and to run the CME's department from there. Perhaps if, upon his appointment, he had decided differently and if he had been prepared to travel to Crewe, closer cooperation could have been forged between the CME's department and the rest of the LMS management, with the possible result that the first LMS Pacific would have been in service by 1927.

So it was that against this background Stanier became CME of the LMS on 1 January 1932. He was faced with problems of a monumental dimension, with pre-Grouping rivalries, particularly in the mechanical engineer's department, a total lack of standardization across the system, and a serious lack of fast and powerful locomotives.

Stanier's engineering and leadership skills enabled him to put into place solutions to these problems. He was able to deal with the disruptions resulting from the major upheaval of the Grouping in a way which stopped the inter-group and inter-departmental wrangling without losing the individual skills and expertise which gave the separate companies within the LMS their special characteristics. He was able to use these skills to focus the different ideas of all the design teams from across the company onto providing the motive power designs which met the requirements of both the travelling public and the financial constraints of the Executive.

Against strong competition from the LNER, with its Gresley Pacifics, the LMS was frankly losing. This was something that Sir (later Lord) Josiah Stamp, President of the Executive, was not prepared to accept, and while the answer was a new locomotive to compete and win against the LNER, the ramifications of that decision were immense. Every part of the company would be affected, from the civil engineer's department via the operations department and signalling to the motive power department. It is significant that the LMS did start to move forward with one accord once Stanier had got into his stride.

To seriously compete against the LNER, the LMS realized early on that a powerful locomotive, capable of continuous steaming over 400 miles or more, with the ability to haul unaided, 500 ton trains over Shap and Beattock Summits, was going to be needed. The 'Royal Scots' were managing the west coast diagrams with a reasonable amount of success, but with no margin for error or any reserve. While there was a degree of pressure to start the design of new locomotives, Stanier believed that it was equally important that the new design should be correct.

Stanier first outlined his ideas for a Pacific class locomotive in April 1932 – three-cylinder and four-cylinder designs were put forward. The three-cylinder version looked much like Hughes' original design except for the boiler. The tender design was a step forward for the LMS, being a resurrection of the tender for the Fowler six-wheel 2–8–2 design, with a 1 ton increase in coal capacity. Although only the final batch of 'Princess Royals' were coupled to the higher-capacity, curved-sided Stanier tenders, the tenders were coupled to all the 'Duchesses'.

The four-cylinder design was finally agreed and the authority to construct the initial batch of Pacifics was given in July 1932. Only three were ordered and of these one set of frames was held back for a further experimental design, ultimately the 'Turbomotive'. The first Pacific, No. 6200, eventually named *Princess Royal*, was completed in June 1933, at a cost of £12,567, including the tender, just eighteen months after Stanier had joined the LMS.

The initial design was similar to that of the GWR 'Kings', which, with Stanier's background, is probably not surprising. The tractive effort was of a comparable 40,300 lb (at 85 per cent boiler pressure (BP)), most of the overall dimensions were identical, and the tapered, originally domeless, boiler clearly showed the Swindon influence. However, there were some significant changes from the 'King' design, such as the independent Walschaerts valve motion for all four cylinders, the introduction of a combined Belpaire and wide firebox (or Wootten firebox) with a larger grate area and a longer boiler (20 ft 3 in as opposed to 16 ft on the

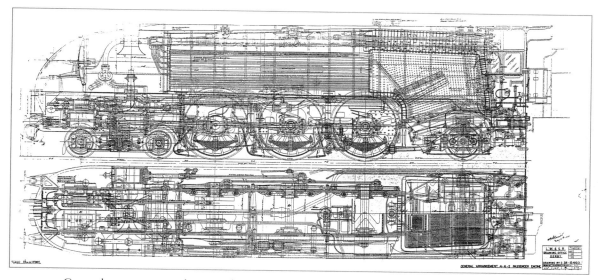

General arrangement drawing for the 'Coronation Scot' locomotives, in single-chimney form. Note Stanier's signature in the bottom right of the drawing, showing his agreement on 9 May 1938.

National Railway Museum, York

'Kings'), the retention of the Derby-type injectors, and of course the addition of the trailing truck. The wide firebox and longer boiler would be particularly useful during the climb on both Shap and Beattock Summits, as well as making sure that the firebox was not choked with clinker at the end of the 400 mile journey.

Initial experiences with the 'Princess Royal' class were not happy, partly because of the inexperience of the crews, who were more used to smaller, less powerful locomotives, but also because of the inherent problems of the original design. Although not fully appreciated at the time, the low-degree Swindon-pattern superheater, coupled with the long boiler barrel, made the locomotives shy on steam, and needing some special coaxing on the part of crews to put in good performances. These problems could be directly attributed to the Swindon influences of the design, and to give Stanier his credit he recognized these failings and was not reluctant to make the necessary changes.

The majority of the final design changes were completed and included on the last and main production batch of locomotives in 1935. The major changes included the doubling of the superheater size, increasing the firebox heating area and adding a combustion chamber which helped to reduce the tube lengths in the boiler. These improvements, coupled with the addition of a steam dome on the top of the boiler barrel, reduced the problems experienced with the locomotives. As crews became more experienced and the new batch entered service some excellent performances were attained. While this may seem a protracted timescale,

No. 6220 *Coronation* on 15 May 1937. Note the original speedometer fittings to the rear driving wheel and the lack of shroud over the top front of the tender.

National Railway Museum, York

one has to remember that electronic design and computer-aided drawing systems were not available. It was time-consuming incorporating hand-drawn design changes, worked out with a slide rule, and to a certain extent a try-it-and-see policy was followed.

The boiler design and crew experiences were to have a large influence on the subsequent design of the 'Duchesses'. One area of potentially disastrous failure was the placing of the outside cylinders over the trailing wheels of the bogie. This caused the cylinders to work loose and strips of metal had to be welded to the mainframes and the cylinders to hold them in place. This was not always successful and the cylinders on the 'Duchesses' were positioned further to the front of the bogie. Another operational problem occurred with the cracking of the rear truck frames; this was never properly cured and was also a typical problem on the 'Duchesses'. A cure was only finally found with the redesign of the truck, when H.G. Ivatt added the postwar standard features to the last two 'Duchesses', built in 1947–8.

In 1938 No. 6205 *Princess Victoria* had the independent valve gear modified by the removal of the inside Walschaerts motion and its replacement with rocking levers operated from the outside valve motion. While this is a case of the 'Duchesses' influencing the subsequent design changes of the 'Princess Royal' class, the addition of rocking levers to the 'Duchesses' arose because of the difficulties in maintenance and servicing of four sets of independent valve motion. One further point which was incorporated in the 'Duchesses' was the use of the bar-framed bogie, which produced significant weight savings on both the 'Duchess' and 'Princess Royal' classes.

During 1936 there was a general increase in the timings on the West Coast Main Line. High-speed test runs clearly demonstrated that a 6 hour schedule could be maintained. While these services were not truly non-stop, consideration was given to the use of corridor tenders similar to those on Gresley's A4s. In fact Stanier designed a corridor tender but it wasn't used consistently in revenue-earning service. A concern was the loss of coal capacity, as it was not unknown for locomotives to be close to, or actually running out of, fuel after a 400 mile run, particularly during bad weather.

With the experience gained from the 'Princess Royal' class with the faster timings on the London to Glasgow runs, it was decided that additional locomotives should be built, based on the 'Princess Royals'. As the initial designs progressed, the development of Stanier's ideas and principles were taken more into account, and as such it was recognized that those Swindon principles which had been proved sound should be continued and improved, but where they had been less than successful on the LMS, they should be discarded. This filtering and refinement of the design produced a brand-new locomotive class very much based on the quality of the 'Princess Royals' but with further improvements in all areas of the design. This new class of locomotive was to be known as the 'Princess Coronation' class, or the 'Duchesses'.

The original intention of the LMS was for the additional locomotives to be improved 'Princess Royal' class Pacifics, but with the various improvements and design enhancements the brand-new 'Duchess' class was authorized by the LMS Board for the building programme of 1937. Initially five locomotives were to be built. Publicly it was expected that the class was to be nothing more than an improved 'Princess Royal' class, and in fact the locomotive committee minutes quoted the numbers 6213–17 for the new Pacifics. It was not until the Company Shareholders Meeting on 26 February 1937 that the LMS announced plans for the high-speed services with new locomotives and coach stock. The new services started revenue-earning traffic on 5 July 1937, with the 'Coronation Scot' hauled by streamlined Pacific, No. 6220 *Coronation*.

The streamlining of steam locomotives had strong commercial advantages. In particular, the Gresley A4s had caught the public imagination in a big way and raised the profile of the LNER considerably. Lord Stamp, President of the Executive, considered that the LMS must compete on equal terms. The initial scheme for the streamlined casing of the 'Duchesses' was set out by Tom Coleman who was then the LMS chief draughtsman. Coleman had been brought in by Stanier when the original chief draughtsman, Herbert Chambers (an ex-Midland man), had disagreed with some of Stanier's early designs. Chambers became technical assistant at Euston.

City of Stoke-on-Trent, No. 6254, still in LMSR livery, entering Euston with the empty stock of the Royal Train on 18 May 1948.

National Railway Museum, York

The streamlined casing was wind tunnel-tested at the LMS research station at Derby and proved as satisfactory as any other shape currently being considered by other companies. While this may sound amateurish compared with today's hi-tech approach, it has to be remembered that the engineering at that time was 'heavy', being designed without the advantage of computers and fluid dynamics, etc. The streamlining turned out to be a genuine aerodynamic shape, in that it caused little disturbance to the air. It was also much more successful than the Gresley A4 shape. The down side to the quality of the aerodynamic shape was the questionable ability to clear steam and smoke from the driver's view, although test results in the wind tunnel did not prove the A4 design to be significantly better.

The effects of streamlining have never been fully quantified using modern methods, and while the debate on the relative merits of streamlining versus conventional designs has continued for many years, it is generally considered that advantage can only be gained with extended high-speed steaming, when the added weight is offset by the aerodynamic improvement. In reality there were limited opportunities in the UK for this type of operation in the 1930s. So while the approximately 2 tons of additional weight could be seen to be an engineering disadvantage, from the commercial and publicity points of view it was a real bonus, raising the profile of the LMS to a high not seen for many a year.

An interesting aside to the subject of streamlining was the positioning of the name-plates of the 'Duchesses' on the middle centre of the streamlined casing, or on the middle centre of the boiler on the nonstreamlined versions. This is different to all the other named Stanier locomotives, where the name is on or close to the centre splasher. While the streamlining forced the change of name-plate position, the change can be considered to add to the stately appearance of these locomotives.

The design of the 'Duchess' class was being planned at Derby during the latter part of 1936 and it was at just this time, November 1936, that Stanier left to take part in a committee of enquiry with Sir Ralph Wedgewood, general manager of the LNER, in India. Without a doubt, while the design principles, layout and general concept were Stanier's, credit must be given to the other members of his team who dealt with the building programme in his absence. Stanier left the overall responsibility of the CME's department in the hands of S.J. Symes, who was the chief stores superintendent, but the responsibility for the detailed design and construction was left in the hands of R.A. Riddles, principal assistant to the CME, and T.F. Coleman, chief draughtsman. The impressive lines of all Stanier's locomotives owe much to the creativity of Coleman and his team. This is particularly so with the scheme and layout for the 'Duchesses', both streamlined and nonstreamlined. Coleman's abilities and skills deserve to be more widely known.

The first five 'Duchesses' were completed at Crewe between June and July 1937. The order of build with costs is shown below:

Number	Name	Date New	Total Cost (£)	Tender Cost(£)
6220	Coronation	June 1937	Averaged across the batch	
6221	Queen Elizabeth	June 1937		
6222	Queen Mary	June 1937	£11,813	£1,556
6223	Princess Alice	July 1937		
6224	Princess Alexandra	July 1937		

These five locomotives were ordered in July 1936 at a quoted cost of £10,400, including the tender. While there is some discrepancy between the ordered estimate and the actual cost, subsequent batches were built well under the quoted cost (see appendices for details). Only after the Second World War did the costs exceed estimates again, which was hardly surprising in view of the delay from quotation to build.

As discussed previously, there were a number of design changes between the 'Princess Royal' and the 'Duchess' classes, primarily as a result of the lessons learnt during operation of the 'Princess Royals'. Principal among the changes was the need to increase the steaming ability of the locomotives, and while the

Duchess of Montrose, No. 6232, at Apsley, with an Up express during 1938, in the original nonstreamlined condition without smoke deflectors and with no break in front of the cylinders. At this time she is still fitted with a single chimney. Note the steam from the coal-pusher at the rear of the tender.

National Railway Museum, York

'Princess Royals' did ultimately produce good steaming results, there were always concerns over a lack of reserve on the long-distance runs. Consequently a complete review of the boiler was made on the 'Duchess' design, where major changes were made compared with previous LMS Pacifics.

The centre line of the boiler from rail level was increased to 9 ft 6 in and the boiler barrel diameter at the smokebox decreased marginally to 5 ft 8½ in. This, coupled with the increase in boiler diameter towards the firebox to 6 ft 5½ in, meant that the overall boiler taper was also increased, given that the boiler length was the same as that of the 'Princess Royals'. The increased barrel diameter and the use of increased diameter driving wheels meant that the firebox front corners were lifted to the extreme limit of the loading gauge. The firebox itself also had an increased fire grate area of 50 sq. ft and the heating surface was increased to 230 sq. ft.

With the increase in boiler size came an increase in the size of the superheater. This was initially 856 sq. ft with forty elements, at that time the biggest superheater fitted to any British locomotive type, although the size was later reduced to 822 sq. ft. The total evaporative heating surface thus became 2,807 sq. ft.

The 'Duchesses' were designed with sustained high-speed running in mind and consequently the diameter of the driving wheels was considered important. At that time locomotive engineering practices decreed that smaller diameter driving wheels were not suitable for sustained high-speed operation, and while it would seem that Stanier himself did not have strong views on the subject, it was Riddles who is on record as having persuaded Stanier to make the change to the 6 ft 9 in diameter driving wheels, a decision it is understood he later regretted. Although the Derby drawing office recognized that a compromise was required for tractive effort and schemed to the next convenient wheel size, which happened to be 6 ft 9 in. It may worth briefly describing how tractive effort is calculated and the significance of the changes made to the 'Duchesses' compared to the 'Princess Royals'. Tractive effort is calculated using the following formula:

$$TE = \frac{P \times D^2 \times S \times 2 \times 0.85}{W}$$

where P is the boiler pressure at 85 per cent, (boiler design assumes that boilers produce 85 per cent of available pressure at any time), D is the diameter of the cylinders, S the piston stroke and W the diameter of the driving wheels. The numeral 2 is the correction factor for four-cylinder locomotives. Consequently it can be readily seen that changes in driving wheel diameter have an immediate effect on the tractive effort; consequently, changes in cylinder diameters or piston

No. 6220 *Coronation*, also known as No. 6229 *Duchess of Hamilton*, just prior to the successful visit to the USA. Note the louvers just behind the front buffers. These were never fitted to No. 6220 *Coronation*!

National Railway Museum, York

stroke would be needed to match original power levels. Piston size and stroke has always been a compromise, with large diameters restricting route availability because of the overall width of the locomotives, while smaller diameters needed faster piston speeds. The optimum stroke length and piston size is a problem that has never been satisfactorily resolved. Although tractive effort does relate to the power classification the latter is also a measure of the boiler efficiency and the braking ability as well. This was shown as a measure of the ability to stop an unfitted freight train. Clearly it was important that a locomotive's ability to haul heavy loads was compared against the same locomotive's power to stop the train!

To keep the tractive effort similar to that of the 'Princess Royals', the cylinder diameter of the 'Duchesses' was increased by $\frac{1}{4}$ in to $16\frac{1}{2}$ in. Similarly, the piston–valve diameter was enlarged to 9 in to allow freer steaming, and the valve travel slightly reduced to $7\frac{1}{32}$ in. The valve motion was reduced from four separate motions to two, with a proportional decrease in maintenance requirements. So as to reduce still further the problems with setting the valve movements, the inside motions were derived from the outside motion via rocking shafts, which were to the rear of the pistons.

A further innovation on the 'Duchesses' was the change in the tender design, which included a steam-operated coal-pusher. This was a significant help to the fireman, considering that he would be likely to move by hand up to 10 tons of coal. The tender interior design was modified to increase the coal capacity to 10 tons from the original 9 tons of the Stanier tenders. The water capacity was not increased above the 4,000 gallons previously carried as it was considered that the number of water troughs on the West Coast Main Line was sufficient for the proposed services (there were eleven sets between Euston and Glasgow).

The total weight of the 'Duchesses' in their streamlined form was 164 tons 9 cwt, as opposed to the 159 tons 3 cwt of the 'Princess Royals', even though the axle weight was the same on the coupled driving wheels. Matching increased power and flexibility without exceeding the weight restrictions was a significant design achievement. All in all the delivery of the first 'Duchess' class locomotives heralded to a new era in railway design and service, and they proved to be powerful, reliable and well-designed engines.

CHAPTER THREE

'DUCHESS' PEOPLE

At the time of the Grouping in 1923 the mechanical engineering department of the LMS was going through a period which could have lead to internecine squabbling between the different groups within the new organization. Over the next eight years, until Stanier took control of the CME's department, there was great internal strife as powerful 'centres of excellence' within the company declined to cooperate with each other.

The other three post-Grouping companies did not have the same difficulties. Gresley was still the CME on the LNER and had been virtually unchallenged since John Robinson of the Great Central Railway stepped down, the GWR was big enough to absorb other smaller companies and still retain its identity, while Maunsell on the Southern had widespread acceptance of his ideas and methods.

The trauma the LMS was suffering was to some extent a result of retirements among the higher levels of management, as much as of deliberate policy. At the time of the Grouping the Midland Railway was by far the biggest of the LMS constituent companies, and the planned structure for the LMS top management included six directors from each of the three largest constituent companies and one from each of the other companies. It was also intended that the other senior management posts would be evenly staffed by officers of all the companies. In 1924 Sir Guy Garnet, formerly of the Midland Railway, became chairman of the LMS and with the retirements noted above, the new company continued the Midland Railway's ethos. This was necessarily a bad thing as sooner or later one of the larger companies would have dominated the new organization, something which is not uncommon in any amalgamation. The problem with the LMS was that this domination was so complete, with any suggestions of non-Midland Railway origin being given little or no credit.

Midland Railway locomotive design did not readily lend itself to widespread use across the LMS system but this was indeed the outcome of early attempts at standardization based on Midland Railway methods of operation. This policy led to a gradual deterioration in the ability of locomotives to cope with the increased speeds and loads required in this new competitive environment. One example was the difficulties experienced with the bearing boxes fitted to the Midland engines. These were very narrow in comparison with other types and were designed so that coupled with the flexibility of frames normally used on Midland locomotives,

No. 6221 *Queen Elizabeth* with the Up 'Royal Scot', passing South Kenton on 27 May 1947. At this time the locomotive is fitted with the sloping smokebox and is still in LMSR livery. From the lack of smoke and steam she seems to be having no problems with the fourteen-bogie load.

National Railway Museum, York

they would allow better running round the tight curves of the Midland system. At that time the Midland Region of the LMS had a poor record of track maintenance and design, so the locomotives were built to accommodate this. Hence, 'Midlandization' brought down motive power qualities to suit the lowest level of track maintenance, rather than improving the track, which was the policy of the other post-Grouping companies. This resulted in the inability to operate more powerful traction at higher speeds.

Clearly, this state of affairs was not popular with the other centres of skilled excellence, in particular Crewe, Horwich and St Rollox, and they decided to bury the hatchet among themselves and turn on the Derby faction. Policy on track design and maintenance, and the problems of partisan management were beyond the control of the CME's department, but it was unfortunately the locomotive designs and operations which were to suffer most. Both Hughes and Fowler were aware of the problems and were constantly thwarted in their attempts to change matters, so much so that in September 1926 occurred what is described by O.S. Nock as 'the most astonishing coup d'état in British locomotive history'.

Fowler had proposed and started to build a new compound four-cylinder Pacific to meet the increased power and load requirements of the LMS, and in fact

No. 46257 *City of Salford* waiting for the guard's signal at Motherwell, while hauling the 09.25 Crewe to Perth service on 30 November 1963. The locomotive was based at Carlisle Upperby (12B) and is shown here in BR green livery.

John Wickham

the mainframes had been cut when the anti-Derby faction made a deliberate attempt to force the hand of the CME. There appeared on the Euston to Crewe route, a GWR 'Castle' class locomotive, No. 5000 *Launceston Castle*. Later the same locomotive appeared on the Carlisle route. Trials were carried out using the mobile test unit and these were to influence future LMS designs. Obviously, a number of people from senior management to shed staff and crews must have been involved for this conspiracy to be so effective. That Fowler was unaware of this was indicative of the widespread ill-feeling within the operating department and the other locomotives centres. Apart from some minor difficulties with the dry sanding system in the high winds and rain on the line north of Preston, the 'Castle' performed well under various operating conditions, so much so that J.E. Anderson, the LMS superintendent of motive power, a man who had very little good to say about anything non-Midland, is quoted as commenting that he 'would not mind having twenty "Castles" for the summer traffic of 1927'. The trials were discussed at the highest level within the LMS, with the result that Fowler's Pacific design was cancelled and a three-cylinder 4–6–0 of comparable design to the 'Castles' was instigated.

At around this time Sir Guy Garnet secured the services of Sir Josiah Stamp as President of the Executive. Garnet had previously reorganized top management so that the Executive consisted of four vice-presidents headed by a president. In 1927

No. 46224 *Princess Alexandra* at Crewe in 1949, still fitted with the sloping smokebox from the streamlined era. The smokebox was replaced during October 1954. The streamlining was removed in May 1946. The locomotive is seen here in BR blue with the British Railways letters across the tender and no emblem.

Rex Conway

Garnet retired and Stamp became both the chairman of the company and President of the Executive. Stamp was well equipped to run the multi-faceted organization, having first-class business acumen and a degree in economics. He was also aware of the problems facing both the operating and the motive power departments, and while the new 4–6–0 'Royal Scot' class was giving reasonable service, as they came nearer the time for heavy repairs, their coal consumption steadily increased. While the solution to this problem was ultimately found to be the addition of the single Schmidt piston ring and a higher boiler pressure, it was obvious that major changes were needed to move the company forward. Stamp knew that without a common design approach and better internal staff relations the whole of the LMS was in jeopardy.

The main problem was having the time to find a replacement CME. In 1930 the first moves to consolidate the long-term success of the LMS motive power department were made. Sir Henry Fowler was appointed assistant to the vice-president for works, a task which allowed him to head up the research side of the operation. On the face of it this move would seem rather harsh, but Fowler was sixty years old and in all probability he and Stamp had discussed the move as a way of getting the locomotive department back on its feet. In any case Fowler was a research engineer at heart and no doubt welcomed his involvement in this side of the industry. Stamp's difficulty was that the natural successor to Fowler was Hewitt Beames who had too many old LNWR allegiances, even though his experience and knowledge were ideal for the task. Beames had extensive experience both as a CME and with the workings of a large engineering organization, having been at Crewe as divisional mechanical engineer. It was Beames who organized the belt system at Crewe, a system which was to be so successful and cost effective in later years.

The new CME had to come from outside the organization, so as to heal the differences, but time would be needed to find the right man and in the short term an interim CME had to be found. The superintendent of the carriage and wagon department, E.J.H. Lemon, was appointed by Stamp, but both knew that this was only a temporary appointment. In fact Stamp already had Lemon in mind to succeed J.H. Fellows, a vice-president due for retirement at the end of 1931. The temporary nature of Lemon's appointment was kept very quiet, so much so that Riddles and his colleagues were less than happy with a carriage and wagon man being appointed CME, feeling it needed a locomotive man. To some extent the outcome of Lemon's appointment was the incorporation of both the locomotive and the carriage and wagon departments within the CME's organization, leading to a more rationalized approach to mechanical engineering in the LMS, a change which assisted Stanier during his time as CME. The situation preceding Stanier's appointment is best illustrated by a comment made by Stamp himself: 'If I'd put a North Western man in they'd have had a banquet at Crewe followed by fireworks in the park. If I'd appointed someone from the Midland all Crewe would have been in revolt. It had to be someone from outside.'

Stanier's appointment on 1 January 1932 was made after a number of informal meetings between Stanier and Lemon, Stanier and Sir Harold Hartley, vice-president of the LMS, and between C.B. Collett, the GWR CME, Sir James Milne, general manager of the GWR, and the GWR chairman Lord Churchill. Collett was told quite firmly by the chairman that he was wanted for the full term as CME, so Stanier, being only five years younger, would have had little chance of gaining that position for long. Thus the stage was set for probably one of the most revolutionary periods of change in the short history of the LMS.

Stanier left the GWR with gestures of goodwill from his management and colleagues, to an appointment on a railway with a totally different method of working and organization. In later years, in conversation with O.S. Nock, he said that his first feeling on being asked to take the post was one akin to embarrassment. On the LMS his mandate was clear: to provide a range of standard locomotives in the lowest number of classes, that could operate over the whole system. Or, to quote Lord Stamp, 'the fewer the number adequate to the task to be performed the more steady, uniform and economic the flow for repairs'. That the mandate was achieved is well-known, but in doing so it led to Stanier's crowning achievement in locomotive engineering, the 'Duchess' class.

It may be thought that details of the growing pains of the LMS have very little to do with the story of the 'Duchesses', but one has to remember that it was out

No. 46237 *City of Bristol* taking water at Carlisle on 2 August 1963. No. 46237 was working the 08.00 Plymouth to Glasgow service. To the right of the 'Duchess' is 0–6–0 tank No. 47515.

John Wickham

of this disunity that Stanier built a team which designed and constructed the 'Duchess' class. This is even more extraordinary considering that Stanier wasn't around much during the initial conception and birth of the class. It has been said that the success of any design is only as good as the people involved with it and in the case of the 'Duchesses' the team was very good indeed.

At the beginning of Stanier's tenure he had the following staff:

Deputy CME	H.P.M. Beames (LNWR)
Personal Assistant to the CME	S.J. Symes (MR)
Technical Assistant and Chief Loco Draughtsman, Derby	H. Chambers (MR)
Works Superintendent, Crewe	F.A. Lemon (LNWR)
Assistant Works Superintendent, Crewe	R.A. Riddles (LNWR)
Works Superintendent, Horwich	R.C. Bond (MR)
Divisional Mechanical Engineer, Glasgow	D.C. Urie (Highland Railway)
Chief Draughtsman, Horwich	T.F. Coleman (North Staffordshire Railway)
Works Superintendent, Derby	H.G. Ivatt (NSR)

Stanier initially made few changes and made full use of the existing engineering expertise, although Stamp would have backed his CME even if he had wanted to make wholesale changes. Stanier was very much of the opinion that respect and confidence could only be achieved with time, and with an understanding of the problems and needs of the organization. This attitude quickly gained respect, amply illustrated by the fact that the motive power superintendent, J.E. Anderson, a constant thorn in Fowler's side, actually got on with Stanier very well. Even with staff who did not like the new ideas, sideways moves were made to change the situation rather than create confrontations. This was particularly true of H. Chambers, the chief draughtsman, a man known to dislike Stanier's methods and not shy of making his opinions of them known. He was eventually moved to Euston and replaced with Coleman, who then became responsible for most of the practical design of Stanier's locomotives.

People who worked for Stanier found him much to their liking and E.S. Cox, ultimately to become executive officer of design for BR, states that while they found him a man of few words, he did not procrastinate and was not doctrinaire, came quickly to the point and made decisions rapidly when presented with the facts. When mistakes were made they were freely admitted and rectifying action ordered. Cox also considered Stanier to be very approachable and someone who would just as freely converse with a fitter, fireman or draughtsman as with the chairman.

Riddles likewise considered his chief easy to talk to and extremely willing to discuss any and all of the problems which were encountered in designing new locomotives. Stanier was further known to explain things which were not understood in detail and with patience, but at the same time he was able to listen and willingly accept the reasoning if it was based on logic.

R.C. Bond also had similar views on Stanier, while E.J. Larkin, who was staff assistant to the CME at the time Stanier retired, had an equally high regard for the man. He quotes an incident that indicates the bonds which developed on Stanier's team. At Stanier's retirement Larkin was called into Stanier's office and told to choose any volume from his bookcase as a memento. This gesture was small in nature but was kind and generous in sentiment. It is highly likely that similar scenes occurred with other members of Stanier's staff.

Two further anecdotes also illustrate Stanier's character. When asked by a one-time 'Duchess' driver why the driving wheels of the Pacific were so large, he commented that it was all to do with the publicity boys. E.S. Cox revealed that Stanier uncharacteristically took great umbrage when claims made by the Ministry of Supply over the new Austerity 2–8–0 seemed to criticize his own 2–8–0 design. He had been seconded to the Ministry at that time and the limited engineering ability of this government department would have probably tried a saint.

The originator and catalyst for the 'Duchess' design was a man who engendered loyalty and respect, and created a bond within the locomotive department which allowed the LMS to eventually lead all the other railway companies in Great Britain in terms of locomotive design. But while the 'Duchesses' were Stanier's concept, the day-to-day design and build were the responsibility of his team.

So who was this team of engineers, many of whom were to become well known in their own right, both during the dying days of the LMS and the steam days of British Railways? At the time of the 'Duchess' design Stanier was in India as part of the Committee of Enquiry for the Indian Government, and consequently the details of the design were left with his 'design team'. During Stanier's absence, S.J. Symes, the chief stores superintendent, was acting CME but it would seem that he was content to allow R.A. Riddles oversee the design work. This was carried out at Derby, where the design and aesthetics were planned out by T.F. Coleman and the drawing office staff. The locomotives were fabricated and assembled at Crewe.

Riddles was principal assistant to the CME at the time of the 'Duchess' design, a position that Stanier himself had held at the GWR. Riddles had been brought up to Euston by Stanier as locomotive assistant to the CME in 1933 and it was during this early period of Stanier's appointment that the loyalty of his department was most needed. Riddles once described his appointment, in a conversation with O.S. Nock, as the 'political agent to the CME'! There was at that time a small minority within the LMS who were keen to see Stanier fail, and it was noted that one senior officer was found referring to Stanier as 'that bloody watchmaker'. This was presumably a reference to comments made by Churchward when praising the quality of the de Glenn compound running gear. It was therefore not a derogatory remark, as was inferred by an officer who should have known better.

The anti-Stanier faction was outside the locomotive department and quick to jump on any shortcomings of the new designs, of which there were a number of opportunities during the early days. Riddles was very much alive to this politicking and made every effort to keep the support for Stanier alive and kicking. One of the many areas where he contrived to reduce the flak was in the instructions issued that neither of the 'Princess Royal' Pacifics, then brand new and suffering early problems with steaming and low superheat, should be taken into the works for repair if the task could be completed in the sheds. R.C. Bond had by this time established a good working relationship with the running staff, to the extent that when a locomotive could be returned to traffic quicker and more effectively by passing it through the works this was done. In the case of 'Princess Royal' class No. 6201 *Princess Elizabeth*, Bond received a very sharp rebuke from Riddles for his pains. Here was a man not afraid to support his boss at no little cost, and somebody who understood Stanier's designs and ideas while at the same time being able to manage and organize the complex processes needed to keep the locomotive department running and to control the construction of new designs. Riddles was ultimately to become mechanical and electrical engineer for Scotland and was finally responsible for the Standard British Railway designs after nationalization. Riddles could be perceived as being ambitious, but it is certainly true that but for his support of Stanier the outcome of this period of LMS history may have been very different.

An atmospheric scene looking towards Edge Hill cutting, as No. 46241 *City of Edinburgh* prepares to leave Liverpool Lime Street station.

David Lawrence, Hugh Davis Collection

Bond was in charge of the building and development of the Research and Testing Station at Rugby, though its operation was delayed because of the Second World War. Previously he had been Works Superintendent at Horwich. When Riddles left the post of Mechanical and Electrical Engineer, Scotland, for government service during the Second World War, Bond took over that post. Ultimately he became Works Superintendent at Crewe at Stanier's behest and then the Mechanical Engineer at Derby, to H.G. Ivatt and finally was Chief Officer (Locomotive Construction and Maintenance, to Riddles) for British Railways.

Interestingly, it is reported that at Sir Nigel Gresley's death in 1941, the LNER chairman, Sir Ronald Matthews, approached the LMS to enquire whether Bond would be available to take on the role of CME for the LNER. At the time no deputy existed and the Board had made no provision for a successor to Gresley. In the event, the enquiries met with little success and Edward Thompson, who was Mechanical Engineer, Southern Area (Western) at Doncaster, became CME of the LNER.

At about this time another member of the 'Duchess' design team became temporarily involved with the LNER, when Thompson instigated an independent review of the Gresley 2-to-1 valve gear. He approached Stanier for assistance, who in turn seconded his chief technical assistant, E.S. Cox. Cox visited Doncaster to examine the situation and in a well-written and argued report he acknowledged that the principles were theoretically correct, but due to service wear in the

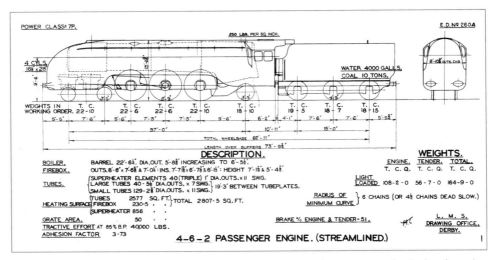

General arrangement of streamlined design for the 'Duchess'. Note the lack of tender shroud and single chimney on the original drawings.

National Railway Museum, York

linkage it would be possible, because of considerably inequality of output between the centre and outside cylinders, for the centre cylinder to develop considerably more power than the outside cylinders. This would apply excessive strain and stresses on the middle big end, producing the danger of serious failures on the road. This was yet another case of the expertise and skills of the 'Duchess' team being acknowledge beyond the LMS.

The design for the 'Duchesses' was schemed at both the Derby and Crewe drawing offices under the control of T.F. Coleman, and in Stanier's absences the responsibility for the aesthetics of both the streamlined and the nonstreamlined members of the class can be credited to Coleman and his team. Coleman had been with the North Staffordshire Railway from 1906 until the Grouping and he remained at Stoke as chief draughtsman until 1926, when he was moved to Horwich. In 1933 he became the chief draughtsman at Crewe. With the departure of Chambers to Euston in 1935, Coleman became the chief draughtsman of the LMS and was based at Derby. He also had technical supervision of the mechanical engineering drawing offices attached to the regions. These were under the day-to-day control of the regional mechanical engineers. The chief draughtsmen at Crewe and Derby were D.W. Sandford and G.R. Nicholson respectively.

Also working at the Derby drawing office at that time was E.A. Langridge, a design draughtsman who must take a significant amount of credit for some of the more detailed laying out of the 'Duchesses'. Langridge had been one of the last apprentices of Mr D. Drummond, CME of the London South Western Railway, entering Eastleigh works in September 1912. He spent a period in the drawing

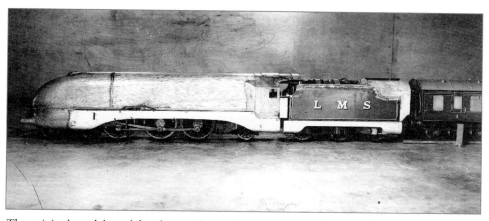

The original model used for the wind tunnel tests to assess the streamlining scheme for the 'Duchess'. The valance on the driving wheels and over the tender has a different shape to the final design; likewise the tender rear extension is more pronounced.

National Railway Museum, York

office there under T.S. Finlayson and then left to join the Midland Railway locomotive drawing office at Derby in 1920. He was put in charge of the LMS locomotive development office under Coleman in 1945, dealing with the final Ivatt designs of steam and diesel locomotives, and then worked on the preliminary designs of the Railway Executive steam locomotives and finally with the British Transport Commission before retiring in 1959.

Thus, by 1936 the design work for the second half of Stanier's tenure was to be under the supervision of a talented and experienced team of draughtsmen who were able to translate ideas and concepts into aesthetically pleasing, efficient and practical designs. The design work was allocated so that the boiler, firebox and other parts above the platform went to Crewe and the balance went to Derby.

Coleman collaborated on the streamlined casing design of the 'Duchesses' with F.C. Johansen who was in charge of the LMS research laboratory in Derby. Johansen was a former National Physical Laboratory (NPL) scientist and would certainly have had knowledge of the results of the previous experimental testing carried out at NPL by the LMS in 1931. The research organization included a small (by today's standards) wind tunnel which, though smaller than the NPL tunnel, was nevertheless able to develop speeds of up to 100 ft per second, or approximately 68 m.p.h. The laboratory was opened on 10 December 1935 by the well-known New Zealand physicist Lord Rutherford. It was within the research laboratory that the streamlining for the 'Duchesses' was tested and finalized.

There has been much discussion on the viability of the 'Duchess' streamlining, and while it is generally accepted that the need for it was almost certainly driven by, the subsequent publicity such a locomotive would attract, and of course Stamp's significant interest in the project, it can also be demonstrated that serious scientific investigations were carried out to produce a design that met both the publicists' and the engineers' requirements. Although the design was developed at Rugby, ultimately the responsibility was Stanier's, and while the design team understood that he was probably less than enthusiastic about streamlining, he was well aware of the advantages claimed by European operators and would therefore make sure that the design was produced according to the best engineering practices.

Johansen's wind tunnel work was carried out using a model of a standard locomotive and one with streamlining fitted. The model was produced so as to allow the standard-shaped boiler to be removed and replaced with a polished wood streamlined alternative upon which different forms of front end could be easily fitted. In addition, the side valances, covers to the cab and tender, and screens for the undercarriage, etc. were tested. Further, the effects of smoke clearance produced by the various shapes were investigated under simulated drifting conditions, as were the problems associated with air currents carrying coal dust into the cab.

Johansen's conclusions were that there were no advantages regarding smoke clearance over the LNER backward-sloping flat front. However, the 'Duchess' shape was the best that could be achieved within the limits of the mechanical design and it was shown to give up to a 20 per cent improvement, aerodynamically, over the LNER shape. This was despite the fact that the LMS design had an air resistance which considerably exceeded that of the 'ideal' locomotive tested previously at NPL in 1931 by the combined LMS/ LNER/Southern Railway team. Johansen went on to suggest a saving in coal costs of between £220 and £300 per annum per locomotive. However, these figures take no account of additional costs for the initial building of the streamlining nor the extra costs associated with its maintenance and servicing. I think these views are somewhat contentious but they are the conclusions drawn at the time by an experienced research scientist.

The results of the investigation into the dust problems on the footplate led to the cover and shroud joining the tender and the footplate roof being fitted with a small upward-projecting lip. This modification was to reverse the flow of air from the tender over the coal and out via the shovelling plate, by creating a flow of air which took the dust out of the cab area away from the crew.

The design of the 'Duchess' class and the trains they hauled attracted exceptional publicity, particularly after the events of the press run when the speed record was obtained, albeit for a short period. This gained the LMS an increased profile and projected the company into the public's imagination. All of this was good for company revenue and increased company awareness, but it also had other effects. Predominant among these was the ability of the LMS to produce something tangible that all the staff of the company could relate to, a success

No. 46240 *City of Coventry* at Willesden shed on 26 January 1964, with 'Jubilee' No. 45672 *Anson* to the left and 0–6–0T No. 47501 to the right. Note the missing shedplate on the smokebox door. At the time No. 46240 was recorded as being a Willesden locomotive, but she had also been sighted with the Crewe North shedplate.

John Wickham

which encouraged pride in the LMS and not one or other of its original constituent companies. The 'Coronation Scot' services united everyone right across the LMS. Staff morale at all levels improved and the company began to provide a higher quality of service with which it could be identified, much the same as that of the original constituent companies.

So who were the people involved in the day-to-day operation of the 'Coronation Scot' trains – the footplate crew, the shed staff and signalmen – and what was it like at the sharp end of these train operations? It was the sheds that were the focal point for all steam operations, including routine maintenance, scheduling of footplate crews, and the servicing and cleaning of all the locomotives. All the sheds were in competition with each other and Camden, particularly during the early 'Coronation Scot' services when all the streamlined locomotives were stabled there, was the great rival of Willesden, which by and large serviced the main-line freight and local passenger services, such as the 'Tring Flier'. When Camden suffered a shortage of crews, men from Willesden were drafted in, which caused great animosity, particularly when a crew from a long-distance freight had to work a streamliner out of Camden. Similarly, Willesden locomotives appearing at Camden were considered inferior and ones to get rid of as quickly as possible.

The top-link crews formed alliances with their home sheds, even though most of the sheds were dirty, uncomfortable, and even downright dangerous. Most train crews would agree that while passengers and enthusiasts look upon the life of the railwayman during the steam era with some romanticism, real life for the staff operating these services was often a hard grind. The LMS provided limited resources compared to today's enlightened views, and yet demanded extreme loyalty for small rewards, other than pride in a job well done.

When the 'Duchesses' returned to Camden shed on completion of the day's 'Coronation Scot' services, they were filled with water and the tenders restocked with coal before undergoing the disposal process. Disposal required two shed enginemen to clear out the fire and get rid of the char in the firebox. The fire was disposed of by one of the men working in the cab while the other worked below the engine in the ashpits. The ashpits were approximately 4 ft deep and, as well as being choked with residual ash removed from previous locomotives, had a skip for the removal of the majority of the ash and clinker. This was a dark and depressing area to work in, not to mention dangerous. The skip was pushed under the firebox of the 'Duchess' and then the shedman in the cab cleared the top layer of hot coals, breaking up the heavy clinker and eventually lifting the firebars sufficiently to allow the firebox to be cleared. The horrors of the ashpit now began as the man beneath the engine started his raking out and called for his mate to open the damper doors. The doors were opened and the ashpan deposited its load into the skip, giving out a mixture of hot dust, clinker, live coals and a shower of sparks. This routine was gone through every time the locomotive returned to the shed and had to be prepared for the next service. Having removed the fire and clinker, the final job was to get rid of any char from the smokebox, a job which provided additional hazards on the 'Duchesses' in their streamlined guise because the casing also had to be opened prior to getting at the smokebox proper. Clearly the shedmen's task was far from pleasant, and it goes without saying that the arrival of the self-cleaning smokeboxes and self-emptying ashpans were welcomed with much relief.

Cleaning the locomotives was another operation with inherent dangers, both from the cleaning materials used and the positions the cleaners had to get in to complete the task. The cleaning crew normally consisted of four cleaners, with the junior member of the team being given the most uncomfortable areas to clean. Typically, a 'Duchess' would be waiting over the pits outside the shed and the junior member would be tasked with cleaning the 'inside' of the streamliner. Issued with a bucket of oil, a scraper and some cotton waste, plus a flare lamp, the cleaner would climb into the guts of the locomotive to commence the cleaning. To reach all the parts of the locomotive entailed climbing over the stretchers, slide bars, brake hangers and axles, and apart from the sweat from the exercise there was also the fear that maybe your mates would forget you and

City of Bristol, No. 46237, seen here in immaculate blue livery at Camden shed on 1 October 1949. The locomotive is obviously still being finished off by the cleaners – note the buckets and cloths on the running plates.

National Railway Museum, York

move the locomotive while you were still underneath. But then, as one cleaner was heard to say, if the senior cleaner had arranged his team to clean this engine he sure as hell wasn't going to get it messy with kids mangled in the big ends! Cleaning the 'Duchesses' was a regular task and the locomotives were always gleaming before the day's operations. The cleaner's job was part of the long and difficult progression to joining the footplate crew of a top-link service.

In the thirties, Camden shed had a staff of approximately a hundred cleaners whose tasks varied from cleaning locomotives to tubing boilers, fire-dropping, steam raising and sandbox filling. Having passed through the various grades of cleaner, passed cleaner and fireman, the next stage was the possible crewing of the top-link express services.

The fireman on main-line services probably experienced the down side of operating over long distances without always receiving the acknowledgements the driver attracted. On the 'Coronation Scot' services it was not uncommon for the footplate crews to have their 'own' locomotive and for both the fireman and driver to be paired on a semipermanent basis. With the pride generated by these services, it was not unusual for the fireman to be at the shed early, before the driver, checking that the steam raisers had given a good start to the fire and steam pressure. He would also make sure that all the locomotive tools were correctly stowed and that his allocation of equipment for the day's service was complete. Having checked that the fire was spread well and the combustion was developing

No. 46224 *Princess Alexandra* hauling the Up midday 'Scot' during September 1959, nearing the summit of Beatock. Clearly the major effort required to deal with this climb has been accomplished as the fireman is having a breather.

National Railway Museum, York

correctly, he would then need to confirm that the water level was correct and the boiler pressure was building up nicely. Next he would check the firebox for damage to the firebrick arch and the tube ends for leaks. Having satisfied himself that the fire could be brought up to full intensity without damage to the firebox or risk to the crew, he would concentrate on bringing both the fire and steam pressure up to meet the driver's requirements.

On the footplate there was only one master, and that was the driver. Sometimes the fireman was unlucky and was paired with a real martinet, while at other times the pairing was amicable though the driver was always the sole commander on the footplate. It was with this in mind that the fireman would make sure that the provision of steam and water for the locomotive was correct and if a problem arose during the build-up of steam pressure, like a sticking damper handle or even the tubes needing blowing out, he would be rushing round to find one of the numerous specialist artisans in the shed to advise on or cure the problem.

The cabs of the 'Duchesses' had been designed with some concessions to the comfort of the crew, both in terms of reducing the draughts and dust, and improving smoothness of the ride, but for all that a footplate of an express locomotive travelling at 70–80 m.p.h. was far from an easy place to stand, let alone work efficiently with a shovelful of coal. Most people would probably be surprised at how cold a footplate could be, particularly at night and when

The 07.13 Workington Main and combined through carriage service from Morecambe Euston Road to Euston hauled by No. 46239 *City of Chester* at Moor troughs on 8 August 1959.

M.H. Walshaw, Hugh Davis Collection

travelling at speed. With the firehole door closed the only heat was that which radiated from the water pipes or escaped from the lagging on the boiler and firebox, and even with the door opened one side of the man was hot while the other side was freezing. To make matters worse, draughts were a constant problem, not only because of the problems of keeping warm but also because of the flying coal dust which got everywhere. A red spotted hanky around the neck, long the fashion for footplate crew, really was the only way to stop the dust getting down the neck, while bicycle clips were worn round the bottoms of overall legs.

During the 'Coronation Scot' service to Glasgow the fireman could move up to 10 tons of coal from the tender to the firebox, and even though the ride was good and the grate was relatively forgiving of how the locomotive was fired, it required a man in good physical condition to meet the demands of the fire, day in, day out. One consolation on the 'Duchesses' was the steam coal-pusher in the tender which at least assisted in bringing the coal forward. This was a major advance, and it is doubtful that some of the prodigious rates of firing mentioned later in this book could have been achieved without this facility.

An additional problem with firing the 'Duchesses' was the quality of coal at various depots around the country. This varied from large slabs (long toms) to the finest of dust (bug dust). The large toms had to be broken by a coal pick, thus added to the bug dust, to a size equivalent to twice a man's fist, and this combination of dust and lumps had to be fed into the fire in a ration of three to one, as both the large lumps and the dust would reduce the white hot fire to a dull red glow with possible disastrous results. While the 'Duchesses' were fairly forgiving in terms of the quality of coal used, it was just one more difficulty to be overcome by the fireman.

In addition to his firing duties, the fireman was also responsible for keeping the footplate clean, operation of the injectors, keeping the water level in the boiler correct at all times, keeping the steam pressure up to the requirements of the road without blowing off (no easy task on the West Coast Main Line with its constantly changing gradients and power requirements) and to note all signals on the fireman's side. All this was done while travelling at speeds on a noisy and draughty footplate.

One other duty of the fireman was the collection of water from the troughs along the road or at any station stops. The filling of the tender tanks was not too difficult using the water towers, in spite of the sliding doors on the streamlined tenders which gave access to the tank fillers, and even in winter when the leather hoses were frozen the task was acceptable. The biggest difficulties came with the collection of water while on the move. At 70–80 m.p.h. it required a high degree of skill to lower the water scoop into the trough at the right time by means of the hand wheel and screw action. Even more adroitness was needed to raise the scoop before the tender tanks overflowed and water streamed back into the leading carriages – something not 'done' on the 'Coronation Scot' services.

Typical of the fireman's skills was the run described previously of the *Duchess of Abercorn* when she produced the highest drawbar horse power ever recorded by operational steam. On 26 February 1939 the fireman, D. Lynn of Glasgow Polmadie shed, was firing at an average of 68.7 lb per mile, which meant that coming over the climb from Motherwell to Beattock Summit, a distance of just over 39 miles, he would have loaded the firebox with 2,717$\frac{1}{2}$ lb of coal in close on 56 minutes, an extraordinary rate of firing, and certainly one that could not be continued indefinitely.

The driver on the 'Coronation Scot' services was very much like the captain of a ship, having absolute power over the footplate and, once on the road, full responsibility for the train and its passengers. The driver on arrival at the shed would check the roster and sign for all the paperwork concerned with the service he was to work, such as speed restrictions, track maintenance, etc. He was expected to be familiar with the whole route that he was to travel and to be aware of all and any changes. Having arrived at the locomotive, the driver would check with his mate to confirm that all the fireman's preparations had been completed with no problems, and then he would move on to checking and oiling round. While different crews had different approaches to preparation, it was unusual for the fireman to be involved in the oiling round. Most crews recognized and appreciated the ease of oiling round on the 'Duchesses', particularly as there was no inside valve gear to be oiled. The crew would move the locomotive out to the station, where the train was connected and the brake and steam pipes tested, and the guard would inform the driver of the load. The signal was then pulled off and the train would slowly move away from the terminus. Thus started three hours of total concentration for the driver on his turn to Crewe.

On the subject of connecting the train to the locomotive, a story is told of a Down 'Duchess'-hauled service climbing to Ruthwell when a travelling ticket inspector noticed that the connecting gangway bellows on a section of the train were somewhat extended. By the time he had informed the guard and the guard had investigated, the train was on the falling gradient past Racks station and no problems could be found. But later, as the driver applied the brakes for Dumfries, part of the train became detached, slowing gently to a halt with the passengers totally bemused as to why the train had come to a stop in the middle of the countryside. Seemingly the shunter at Carlisle Citadel station had connected the bags and all of the pipes but had forgotten to connect the screw coupling!

The system which produced drivers in the heyday of steam was hard, brutal and anachronistic, but that it produced the skills and expertise required to drive an express train over many miles safely in all conditions was not in doubt. The drivers knew the road like the backs of their hands, and were able to pinpoint exactly where the train was in any conditions by the sounds, the smells and the scenery. They were able to name every signal on the road and know what was coming ahead by the bridges, viaducts and crossings, etc., experience that was gained over many years and something which engendered a quiet pride.

The driver was of course exposed to exactly the same conditions as the fireman during the journey, and the footplate camaraderie developed into some long-lasting friendships, with great respect given for the other's task. Yet during the prewar streamliner services the relationship between driver and fireman was very hierarchical and any attempt to challenge this during the journey would be less than popular. It was unusual for the driver to lend a hand at firing at this time, although this was to become more common in the later years of steam. At the end of the run it was the driver who got first go at the bucket of hot water in order to clean up prior to arriving at the shed, and likewise the driver who was responsible for signing off the locomotive and reporting any faults prior to leaving the shed for either the lodgings or the mess room to await the return journey.

The 'Duchess'-powered streamlined trains were very special and had to maintain a very high standard in terms of service to the passenger. It was on the train where the passenger guard ruled supreme. The passenger guard, although smartly uniformed with a carnation or other flower in his buttonhole and brightly polished shoes, was in fact a lesser mortal than, say, the guard of a fitted freight train, who was capable of working both freight and passenger trains whereas a passenger guard could only guard the latter. However, the passenger guard was a formidable character, at the peak of his career, with responsibility for on-time departures and assisting the driver with all safety aspects of the train and ascertaining that the loading was correct and within limits.

It was the guard, with his company-issued pocket watch, who logged all the running times, both overall and point-to-point. His logs would be examined by

No. 46237 *City of Bristol* at Euston during the early fifties.

Bob Barnard, Hugh Davis Collection

the company officers for desultory running and any bad timekeeping. Any examples of bad timekeeping would be recorded against both the driver and the locomotive shed. No doubt this was considered harsh by the footplate crews, particularly when permanent-way restrictions were imposed, and doubly so if the lost time had been made up at the end of the journey but was still held against the crew because of a late point-to-point timing. For all that, it has to be remembered that train movements were extremely complicated and any delays could cause knock-on effects across the whole system. On the 'Coronation Scot' services late running could have been disastrous, as special efforts were already being made to keep the route clear for them.

The guard was also the main point of contact with the passengers, and it was the guards who became well known to many regular travellers. They became in some respects a guide, a friendly face, an adviser and a general assistant to help solve all the little problems of the journey. It was the guard, who through his attitude and demeanour in dealing with the travelling public, helped to raise the service on the 'Coronation Scot' to a higher level than had previously been attained. Services included meals at your seat and, for first-class passengers, full silver service, all served by well-trained liveried stewards. Passengers had large comfortable seats from where they could appreciate the luxury décor which fully reflected the style and exuberance of the time.

No. 46230 *Duchess of Buccleuch* exhibiting volcanic effort as she storms up from Beattock station with a heavy load during August 1956. Note the banking from the rear.

National Railway Museum, York

While it is generally supposed that the footplate crew is the 'King of the Road', signalmen would normally dispute this and during the time of steam believed that drivers and firemen were chosen for their brute strength just as much as the ability to drive the locomotive. The signalman believed that the majority of the safety requirements of the road were his responsibility and that the driver had to obey the information presented by him. Without wanting to get into a dispute between the footplate and the signal-box, suffice to say that the signalman had to display a high degree of responsibility for the safety of the section he was controlling. Signalmen were governed by numerous rules which became more complex as their careers progressed, and additionally any mistakes were recorded in most cases by block and signalling instruments for all to examine.

The signalman's work is controlled by intricate rules and regulations covering the eventualities of both normal and emergency working. These rules form part of the examinations which are the basis for progress to the higher grades and for the signalman to continue his job on an annual basis. Signal-boxes are normally sited at complex track layouts or at track section boundaries, and in either case the signalman has enormous responsibility both for the safe transit of all trains and for the sorting of trains in the section so as to minimize delays caused by slower goods and passenger trains to the fast main-line express services.

The signal-box was a restricted area and was normally kept in pristine condition, with the brasswork, windows and woodwork shining and well polished. Signal staff were a fastidious bunch of people, and were consequently very particular about who could visit the box, particularly if it was a sooty engineman in big scruffy boots and greasy overalls. The relationship between signalmen and footplate crews was normally friendly because of the reliance they each had on the other's expertise and knowledge. However, there were times when a peace offering would have to be made to the signalman if a small misdemeanour occurred, such as slightly overrunning a signal when the rails were particularly greasy and wet, in which case some coal would be left by the track side to be retrieved later by the signalman, or the fireman would bring a driver's hand cloth for use with the signal levers. Both would be very welcome at the box, particularly the former if the box was in an isolated area and there was cold weather.

It was against this background that the signalmen had to deal with the additional problems of the high-speed 'Coronation Scot'. Trying at all points to make sure that the streamliner had precedence over the other services wasn't something that was always successful. Trains could be slowed on the approach to home signals because the preceding train was delayed and not yet out of section, or goods trains would be slow in pulling into sidings or passing loops, and all these and more had to be dealt with by the signalman while under pressure by control to keep the 'Coronation Scot' on time and on the move. One can imagine the anxiety of the signalman in his box awaiting the bell code to tell him the previous train is out of his section while at the same time wanting desperately to pull the signals off so that the rapidly approaching streamliner will not be forced to slow down or come to a complete stop.

These were the men who by hard and sometimes dangerous work provided one of the best railway services of the time, if not of all time. It was the railwaymen who enabled the streamlined 'Coronation Scot' services to show off to the full the power and style of these great 'Duchess'-hauled trains.

DESIGN AND CONSTRUCTION

The 'Duchess' design can be considered to be the peak of the engineering abilities of the CME's department under Stanier, and though he was in India for most of the design and build stages, his influences can be clearly seen. Admittedly Stanier had a difficult time with some of his initial locomotive designs but it was because of his ability to be flexible, and to take sound engineering principles and carry them forward, recognizing and discarding ineffective ideas, that enabled the 'Duchesses' to be successful. The 'Duchess' design was derived directly from the 'Princess Royal' Pacifics and originally it was considered that the new locomotives for the west coast service would be nothing more than improved 'Princess Royals'. But as Stanier and his team compared the requirements for the new service with the problems and areas of unreliability of the earlier Pacifics, it became apparent that a different design was going to be needed if the full benefits of the new train were to be met.

That the 'Duchesses' were different was obvious from their original streamlined casing. However, a scheme had been put forward to streamline the 'Princess Royal' class in March 1935, when wind tunnel tests were carried out. The design was similar to German thinking of this time. The German railways had a number of rounded, streamlined locomotives in service. Comparisons between the LMS Derby drawings do show a similarity with the final designs of the 'Duchesses', particularly the fully rounded front aspect of both schemes.

The LMS was no newcomer to the idea of streamlining locomotives, having commissioned the National Physical Laboratory in 1931 to research the effects of air resistance to trains on behalf of the LNER and the Southern Railway which contributed to the costs. Details of these tests and the results of the research were not published until 1936, with illustrations appearing in the *Proceedings of the Institute of Mechanical Engineers*, Vol. 134. These showed that a scale model of a 'Royal Scot' 4–6–0 had been wind tunnel-tested. The tests were completed with three different streamlined shapes on the 'Royal Scot' model, one fully encased with a wedge-shaped frontal area, another with only a domed extension to the smokebox, similar to GWR streamlined designs, and one with no embellishments at all. It is interesting that the wedge shape did produce improvements but was not considered for any future LMS schemes. The conclusions recommended some caution on the use of the data, as a whole streamlined train would have to be

Coronation, with all wheels and the streamline casing almost complete, Crew, 10 May 1937.

National Railway Museum, York

operating to maintain the results rather than just a streamlined locomotive. In addition, full consideration of the effects of sidewinds would need to be taken into account. Clearly, by the time the results were published, designs for the 'Duchesses' were well advanced and moving in a different direction to that originally proposed.

At about the same time, other streamlined express services were developing in Germany, the United States and France, and in fact the French were running comparative trials with steam- and diesel-hauled trains. Interestingly, the diesels were based on the Bugatti sloping-fronted railcar, similar to the design used by Gresley for his A4 Pacifics. The steam-powered Atlantic 4–4–2 locomotives used for the trials were designed with a rounded front, not unlike the 'Duchess' design. The trials showed that steam locomotives could meet, and could continue to meet, the exceptional speed and service demands required of the diesel railcar services, with far more commodious accommodation. At one stage, a comparison between nonstreamlined and streamlined steam locomotives of the same class, hauling identical train loads, was made. It was discovered that it was possible for a streamlined train to save up to 450 hp when travelling at 87 m.p.h. Stanier considered that the results of these trials indicated that streamlining could save up

Piston and valve chest details viewed from the front of the locomotive, showing the cutaway of the curved front of the running boards, allowing easier access to the pistons. This was part of the modifications completed at the time the 'Duchesses' were 'defrocked'.

Author's Collection

to 28 per cent of coal consumption and 23 per cent of water under constant high-speed conditions, figures which would have a significant bearing on West Coast Main Line services. However, it was felt that Stanier was not really keen on streamlining at all.

The 'Duchesses' were schemed out and designed at the LMS Derby and Crewe drawing offices, with most of the detailed work credited to T.F. Coleman, the chief draughtsman of the LMS. Also at Derby was the company's scientific research laboratory, which included a wind tunnel. This was the only one in existence within any of the four railway companies. The laboratory was set up by a former NPL scientist, F.C. Johansen, and opened in December 1935.

Having schemed out the initial streamlined design it was wind tunnel-tested at the laboratory until the final design gave both practical and aerodynamic success. In later discussions about the streamlining of the 'Duchesses' there is some criticism of the use of this shape, particularly when the previous National Physical Laboratory results indicated a wedge-shaped front. Critics would say that the design was dictated more by publicity requirements than genuine engineering results. In some respects this is a valid criticism but it should also be remembered that Stanier was influenced very much by the experiences of the French and German railways who already had similar fully rounded designs. In addition, the shape was wind tunnel-tested to show that evidence was available to satisfy the design criteria. And even if there was undue influence from the publicity department, the concept and results were more than satisfying for the whole of the LMS.

No. 46257 at Carstairs, showing some motion details and the name-plate, on 9 November 1963. Note the hollow axles.

John Wickham

There has been much debate on the value of streamlining over the years, and whether the additional weight and maintenance problems were rewarded by lower running costs. It is difficult to discover empirical evidence to prove or disprove the use of streamlining but I think it is significant that any serious trial always made the point of stating that the results were dependent on continuous high-speed running, typically 75–90 m.p.h., and the French trials clearly state the results were valid at 87 m.p.h. With the streamlined 'Duchesses' weighing nearly 3 tons more than the nonstreamlined versions, and with the limited route miles where trains could travel at speeds in excess of 70 m.p.h., I leave the reader to make their own assumptions on the technical validity of streamlining. One interesting side issue in the discussion on the viability of streamlining was the fitting of 'winged' headlights on the buffer shanks of the streamlined members of the class. The look was certainly innovative but whether this embellishment gave any additional aerodynamic advantage is highly doubtful.

Stanier is quoted as saying in his 1936 Institution of Locomotive Engineers Presidential Address that 'streamlining may be something like that blessed word Mesopotamia to the old lady. At any rate it has good publicity value.' In his biography of R.A. Riddles, Rogers states that Stanier loathed streamlining. Such comments can only be assumed to be directly attributable to Riddles himself.

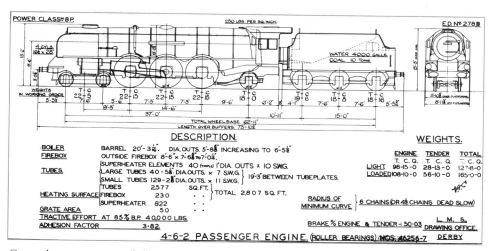

General arrangement of the Ivatt-modified 'Duchesses', Nos 46256 and 46257. Note the cutaway in front of the cylinders, the shortened cab side sheets and the changed pony truck design.

National Railway Museum, York

One of Stanier's major steps forward was his firm belief in stationary testing plants and that only in those could the differences of locomotive condition, weather and the road be isolated. With this in mind, the joint testing station at Rugby was started by both the LMS and LNER in 1938. The enthusiasm Stanier exhibited in his cooperation with Gresley in setting up the test plant indicates the importance he felt about such matters. This was all in strong contrast to his comments in 1931 when, discussing a Gresley paper called 'Locomotive Testing Stations', he expressed serious doubts about the benefits of static test plant. This attitude was probably the result of his experience of static testing at the GWR test station. The Swindon-based plant had limited power-absorbing capability and was known to have given problems in use, so it was probably not unreasonable for Stanier to express his doubts. Even so, at that time Stanier had more experience of static testing than any of the other CMEs of the 'Big Four'. It was on the Rugby test plant in 1956 that No. 46225 *Duchess of Gloucester* achieved the ultimate performance of the class, producing a steam rate of 40,000 lb per hour, probably the highest-ever rate of steam production for a locomotive in Great Britain.

One of the major locomotive engineering design changes of the interwar years was the introduction of the Pacific or 4–6–2 wheel arrangement. All of the pre-nationalized railway companies had one or more Pacific designs, except the GWR, which apart from one experiment still retained large 4–6–0 designs based on the original ideas of Churchward and Collett. It was, of course, the LNER Pacifics which precipitated the LMS Pacific design.

The Pacific wheel arrangement originated in the United States in 1886, when George S. Strong designed a 4–6–2 locomotive which was built at Wilkes Barr and ran on the Lehigh Valley Railroad. The success of the Pacific wheel arrangement in Britain was due to its ability to enable a truly flexible design to be built which would meet the particular variations of the different route restrictions of the British network, while at the same time producing the power and versatility required for both the high-speed, long-distance express and fast goods services of the day. In particular, the use of six coupled wheels, arranged fairly closely together, with a leading bogie and trailing truck, allowed the maximum size boiler and firebox within the loading gauge and also produced good ride and stability. However, one problem associated with the Pacific wheel arrangement was a lack of sure-footedness when starting with heavy loads, causing slipping, which was particularly apparent with the Bulleid Pacifics of the Southern Railway before they were modified. Slipping was due in part to the proportion of the total weight carried on the trailing truck and was never satisfactorily solved, even on the final BR Standard designs.

The Pacific arrangement on the 'Duchesses' enabled the accommodation of a wide Belpaire firebox, sometimes referred to as a Wootten firebox, joined to the optimum boiler size and shape for free steaming, a prerequisite for long-distance high-speed running. A simple rule of thumb for freedom of boiler steaming is the measure of the total of free area through the boiler tubes taken as a percentage of the firebox grate area, typically 14 to 15 per cent is considered good.

Two main advantages are claimed for the Belpaire firebox: its better steam generation, due to a greater firebox heating surface in contact with the water, and the addition of more space above the firebox for water and steam. Further, the design allows heavy girder stays, common in round-topped fireboxes, to be dispensed with. These stays were known to be unsatisfactory because, in a round-topped firebox, when the boiler is heated the uneven expansion of the copper firebox in relation to the steel wrapper can leave the front part of the inner box unsupported. During heating, the large flat crown plate of the Belpaire firebox deals with thermal expansion more easily and consequently the roof stay problems are reduced. In addition, two flat surfaces are easier to stay than one round and one flat surface. Against these advantages must be put a small increase in manufacturing and maintenance costs, but the locomotive was designed for long, hard workings and consequently an increase in steaming ability outweighed any of the disadvantages.

In view of the requirements for high speeds, the coupled wheel size was increased to 6 ft 9 in from the 6 ft 6 in of the 'Princess Royal' class, as this was the next standard tyre size. The intention was to use the largest boiler possible within the loading gauge, with the largest convenient size of driving wheel. As the cylinder stroke was the same for both the 'Duchesses' and the 'Princess Royals', the cylinders were increased in diameter by $1/4$ in to $16^1/2$ in, thereby keeping a similar tractive effort on each class. The firebox and cab were supported by the rear Bissel truck which was anchored some 6 ft 10 in ahead of the truck axle centre line.

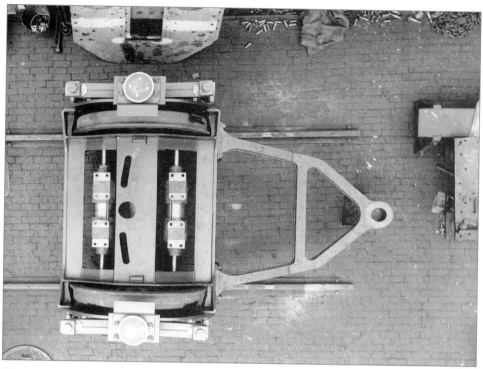

The original pony truck as fitted to the 'Duchess' class, except for the Ivatt-built members of the class. This truck is waiting at Crewe on 30 April 1937 to be fitted to No. 6220 *Coronation*.

National Railway Museum, York

Stanier recognized that ride was an important factor and decided that to cope with the speeds expected and to create the required stability, a four-wheel bogie truck was needed to lead the locomotive into curves and crossings. This was similar to that fitted to the 'Princess Royal' class, including the bar frames, but with some improvements, in particular being better able to deal with the effect of the lateral forces on the track created by the locomotives. This effect was as much, if not more, important than the hammer blow caused by the vertical forces of the reciprocating parts of the engine.

Experiments revealed that the object of bogie wheels is not only to relieve the extreme flange forces on the leading driving wheels when going into curves, but also to reduce the effects of oscillation and the resulting flange forces while on straights. The original pony truck design on the 'Princess Royal' class had already achieved adequate side control by the use of springs and constant friction control, but on the 'Duchesses' Stanier insisted that, in addition, the bogie and pony truck axleboxes should be maintained to an extremely high standard. Further, the leading bogies and trailing trucks were designed with thicker wheel flanges to

The front bogie of No. 6220 *Coronation* at Crewe during May 1937. On the right can be seen the buffers and front of No. 6220, and in the background the driving wheels of an unknown 0–8–0. Note the bar frames of the bogie.

National Railway Museum, York

reduce the clearances between wheel and rail, and increase the time between shop visits for flange wear. Side control can only be effective after side clearance between axlebox and horns, wheelboxes and axlebox, and wheel flange and rail have been taken into account. The bogie side movement was $2\frac{3}{4}$ in either way and the loading normally given as 4 tons initial and 5 tons final, while the pony truck had $4\frac{1}{4}$ in either way with 1.44 tons initial and 2.96 tons final loading.

An additional difference between the 'Princess Royals' and the 'Duchesses' was the use of hollow crank axles. This idea, taken from the GWR, was not just meant to save deadweight but also to produce better performance by heat treatment of the outside surface of the crank axles. Unfortunately, technology was such that heat treatment was not able to deal satisfactorily with the insides of the axles and consequently all the axles were bored out. The bogie axles had a 2 in hole, the leading coupled wheels and Bissel truck axles a 3 in hole, and the intermediate and trailing coupled wheels $4\frac{1}{2}$ in giving a total saving of 9 cwt. While this saving was significant, Stanier himself said that 'this weight saving was a bonus'.

Name-plate details of *City of Carlisle*, 23 February 1964. Note the hollow axle for the main driving wheels.

John Wickham

The whole emphasis of the design of the 'Duchess' was for operating sustained, high-speed, long-distance express diagrams, and as a result a delicate balance existed between the need for power, efficiency and free steaming, and the need to keep axle loadings to a minimum. Consequently, serious efforts were made to reduce weight across the whole design. Significantly, the maximum axle loading, at 20 ton 10 cwt, was exactly the same as the 'Princess Royals', even though the overall weight of the 'Duchesses' was increased by some 5½ tons.

Part of this overall weight reduction could be seen in the design of the frames, for which a special steel was chosen, allowing a reduction of ⅛ in thickness. The steel was of a grade containing 0.2 per cent carbon, 0.85 per cent manganese and 0.45 per cent chromium, with minute quantities of other elements. The composition of the steel was reached after detailed research into its suitability for welding, gas cutting and strength. The result was a stronger material, which avoided the problems of excessive local hardening when being cut or welded. Notwithstanding the research, special processes still had to be applied when cutting or welding, including preheating areas, retempering edges with a blowpipe, and cutting and welding at slower than normal speeds. Any indications that these procedures caused problems during the fabrication of the frames or in the later life of the locomotive are difficult to quantify.

Frames of No. 6220 *Coronation* at Crewe in April 1937, showing the cylinders and valves fitted without cladding. Note the boiler saddle seen protruding above the frames at the front.
National Railway Museum, York

The frame plates were similar in outline to those on the 'Princess Royal' class, having a rear extension with both inner and outer frames. The mainframes were braced by the front buffer beam and the dragbox, with additional stretchers consisting of the inside cylinders, smokebox saddle, two vertical stretchers between the driving wheels, and a stretcher at the junction of the rear frame extensions. This latter also provided the bearing pivot for the Bissel truck. Bearing surfaces were fitted for the boiler support saddles, to allow for thermal movement of the boiler. A main sliding support at the front of the foundation ring was schemed out by L. Barraclough, originally from Horwich and then the Crewe drawing offices. The design was based on that used by the North British Locomotive Company for its Indian State locomotives. The base of the foundation ring rested on a shoe which was free to slide longitudinally but not transversely. The rear extension overlapped the mainframes on both the inside and outside and was braced by a stretcher above the Bissel truck axle between the inner frames. Each pair of plates was also braced by a stretcher which included the Bissel truck side bearers, the rear dragbox and buffer beam.

The drawgear and buffers were of standard LMS type, as were the springs, which were silico-manganese laminated steel plates attached to the axleboxes and spring hangers in a similar manner to those on the 'Princess Royal' class. There

Detail of the valve rocking shaft from which the inside valve motion was derived. The rocking shaft is mounted to the rear of the valve chest.

Author's Collection

was a relatively high mortality rate for road spring failures on both the 'Princess Royals' and the 'Duchesses', and this was later found to be because of the method of manufacture. The spring sections were rolled, not machined, and after heat treatment were hammered into shape. This resulted in increased stresses on the springs during the process, with a consequent higher risk of failure. The axleboxes and horn guides were also similar to the 'Princess Royals' and lubricated in the same way.

The 'Duchesses' were built as four-cylinder locomotives, driving the centre coupled wheels from the outside cylinders and the leading coupled wheels from the inside cylinders. They were fitted with two sets of outside Walschaerts valve gear, with the inside valve motions derived from the outside via rocking shafts. This was the reverse of GWR practice, where the outside motion was derived from the inside valve gear. The rocking shafts were positioned to the rear of the steam chest, immediately above the slide bars, and were connected to the valve spindle forward of the combination lever. This arrangement meant thermal expansion did not have an undue effect on the settings of the inside valve motion. In addition, this design also contributed to the weight reduction and made the valve gear more accessible, with less likelihood of in-service problems. A problem with the valve motion of the 'Royal Scot' locomotives was that occasionally the radius

Valve and piston motion details, showing the piston rod, slide bars, cross head, combination lever, union link, connecting rod and radius rod.

Author's Collection

rod hit the expansion link when the driver was using full gear while coasting. As the 'Duchess' gear was similar to that on the 'Royal Scots', a better design was needed, which was schemed out by D.M. Wilcox from Horwich. A lighter-pattern girder with plummer blocks was designed to carry the expansion links. A large-diameter hollow-bored reversing shaft was arranged at the rear end with a bell crank of which one arm carried the sliding block in the radius extension and the other arm connected to the reversing screw. On the right-hand end one arm only was fitted for connection to the sliding block.

The outside connecting rods were each some 7 lb lighter than those fitted to the 'Princess Royals', even though they were 2 ft longer, and this was achieved by the use of a stronger grade of steel. The fluted-section coupling rods were also made of the same grade of steel and savings of 412 lb were made over all the rods. In addition to actual weight saved, significant savings in reciprocating weight were made. The reciprocating weight per cylinder was 640 lb compared with 715 lb for the 'Princess Royals'. The hammer-blow for the 'Duchesses' was 1.31 tons for each pair of coupled wheels and 0.24 tons for the locomotive. This converts to five revolutions per second, or just over 23 m.p.h.

The cylinders had inside steam admission and for the 'Duchesses' were set, both inside and outside, at an inclination of 1 in 50, and constructed from cast iron

Details of the front bogie bar frame. Note also the position of the valve and piston chest relative to the bogie.

Author's Collection

with the same stroke as the 'Princess Royals'. From 1952 the cylinders were replaced, upon renewal, with cast steel fitted with cast-iron liners. Steam passages were designed to provide the freest steam flow. The valves were enlarged to 9 in diameter from 8 in and the piston heads had reduced-thickness webs, which also saved weight. The steam passages were very direct and internally streamlined, but in the case of the exhaust steam passages were not so enlarged as to cause them to act as receivers. The straight ports of the cylinders were a great worry for the foundry during production, as the straight walls could become stressed between the body of the cylinder and that of the steam chests when cooling off after casting, and flaws were not unknown. Piston valve heads were also streamlined in the body, having a false cover on the outer sides.

The importance of internal streamlining was fully recognized by Stanier and his team, to the extent that a special engineering rig was designed to test the effects of different forms of internal streamlining. It was shown that at exhaust an 18–37 per cent reduction and at admission an 0–18 per cent reduction in resistance to steam flow could be achieved. Stanier, during his Presidential Address to the Institution of Locomotive Engineers in 1939, acknowledged the considerable influence of André Chapelon, who had alerted the engineering community to the importance of internal streamlining for steam locomotives.

DETAILS OF VALVE MOTION, WHEEL AND BOILER RELATIVE DIMENSIONS

	'Princess Royal'	'Duchess'
Cylinder diameter	16¼ in	16½ in
Stroke	28 in	28 in
Coupled wheel diameter	6 ft 6 in	6 ft 9 in
Boiler pressure (psi)	250	250
Tractive effort at 85 per cent boiler pressure	40,300 psi	40,000 psi
Piston valve diameter	8 in	9 in
Maximum valve travel		
Inside	7¼ in	7¹/₃₂ in
Outside	7⁵/₁₆ in	7¹/₃₂ in
Steam lap	1¾ in	1¾ in
Exhaust clearance	Nil	¹/₁₆ in
Lead	¼ in	¼ in
Cut-off in full gear	73½ per cent	75 per cent

The small exhaust clearance on the 'Duchesses' was significant to the increase in free steaming but as noted earlier the most important contribution to the steaming capability was the increase of the valve diameter from 8 in to 9 in.

The exhaust from all four cylinders, in the original design, was combined at a single blastpipe with a 5¾ in nozzle, which was approximately 3 ft below the single chimney throat. Numbers 6220–34 were so built but after trials and a near-disastrous run by No. 6234, a double blastpipe and chimney were fitted. The run by No. 6234 *Duchess of Abercorn*, fitted with a single blastpipe and chimney, took place in February 1939. She was coupled to a 600 ton train and when travelling over Shap and Beattock the boiler pressure fell dramatically and she was unable to keep time. A repeat journey some two weeks later over the same route with the same loading, but this time fitted with a double chimney and blastpipe, produced the historic run when 2,510 drawbar horse power was achieved, a figure never exceeded by any British Pacific locomotive (more details of this run can be found in Chapter Five). All future 'Duchesses' were then fitted with a double chimney and blastpipe and the earlier locomotives modified at convenient maintenance periods.

The double blastpipe and chimney consisted of two 4⁷/₁₆ in nozzles placed 1 ft 3 in below the boiler centre line. The main advantage of a double blastpipe and chimney is that of doubling the surface area of the exhaust cone and therefore improving the draught, particularly when the locomotive is working at short cutoffs with a soft blast. Similarly, by increasing the area of the blast orifice, a more rapid release of spent steam to the chimney occurs, thus reducing back pressure which significantly improves the free steaming at speed.

Interestingly, No. 6245 *City of London* was fitted at one stage with a Kylchap exhaust system. The origins of this change are difficult to ascertain but it is possible that it may have originated from the Doncaster Works of the LNER and, at one stage, that the Kylchap exhaust system was also in the hands of the

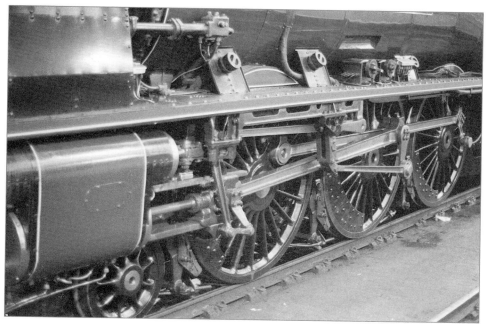

Motion details, showing the reversing gear, eccentric rod and eccentric crank. Note also the brake assembly and the sanding pipes to supply the driving wheels.

Author's Collection

Southern Railway's Eastleigh Works. In any case, it is recorded that when asked by a senior LMS official why *City of London* was making a different exhaust noise from the rest of the class, the modification was removed.

As has already been discussed, the earliest designs for the 'Duchesses' were just enhancements of the 'Princess Royal' class, but even at that stage it was recognized that changes to the boiler were needed to meet the new service demands. At one stage a water tube firebox-type boiler was postulated, though this idea was soon discarded. As the requirements changed, the boiler was completely reviewed and an almost complete redesign was carried out.

The boiler was somewhat larger than that fitted to the 'Princess Royals'. The front diameter was the same, but it was $2\frac{1}{2}$ in wider at the firebox throatplate. The boiler had 13 sq. ft more heating surface and the firebox grate an additional 5 sq. ft. The boiler barrel and firebox wrapper plates were constructed of 2 per cent nickel steel, which allowed the barrel and plates to be up to $\frac{3}{16}$ in thinner than the normal carbon steel, with a subsequent weight saving of 2 tons $3\frac{1}{2}$ cwt. The firebox itself was constructed in the standard manner using copper.

The boiler barrel on the 'Duchesses' was a frustum of a cone, in that it tapered continuously to the smokebox on both the top and underside of the barrel. This was different to the 'Princess Royals', whose boilers only tapered at the top, and

No. 6229 *Duchess of Hamilton* at Crewe in August 1938. She stands as yet unpainted or coupled with her tender, but fitted with the name-plate, also in the unpainted state. Alongside is the 0–4–2 *Lion* of the old Liverpool and Manchester Railway.

National Railway Museum, York

also the previous Stanier taper boilers with parallel front and back rings. Crewe drawing office had pointed out previously the advantages in manufacture of a conical boiler barrel and with this design the full benefits were gained. The arguments for a true conical boiler are based on the fact that the hot gases from the firebox lose heat as they move further from the fire. Consequently, it is more efficient to taper the boiler towards the front so that the heat is progressively concentrated as the gases move towards the smokebox. In addition, there was a weight saving at the front end of the boiler which offset the increase in weight from the Wootten combined Belpaire/wide firebox fitted to the 'Duchesses'. The tapering boiler also added to the handsome appearance of the locomotives.

The disadvantages of conical boilers are the additional manufacturing costs and the increased difficulties in construction, but in view of the favourable comments Stanier made about Crewe's boiler shop abilities, construction was not a problem. The increased efficiency gained from such a boiler design was particularly advantageous in locomotives working hard for long periods, typical of the services the 'Duchesses' were to operate. Consequently, any disadvantages of cost or manufacture were more than offset by the advantages.

The front tubeplate was set back $7\frac{1}{8}$ in into the barrel, while the throatplate consisted of a top and bottom section. The top section of the throatplate joined

No. 6220 *Coronation*, complete with the special rake of coaches for this service, hauling the Down 'Coronation Scot' from Euston to Glasgow, passing South Kenton on 14 July 1937. Note the winged headlamps and single chimney.

National Railway Museum, York

the barrel to the firebox wrapper and formed the shoulders for the combined wide/Belpaire firebox, while the bottom formed part of the combustion chamber extension to the firebox. The joint between the wrapper and the throatplate was at an angle of approximately 60 degrees. The firebox was designed to the greatest width possible, 7 ft 9 in at the throatplate tapering to 6 ft 11^1/$_{16}$ in at the footplate end. The firebox wrapper was of one single plate. The foundation ring to the barrel gave a water space of 3^3/$_4$ in all round the firebox.

The firebox was 8 ft 6 in long with the grate having a vertical drop of 1 ft 4 in. The level section at the backplate was 2 ft 11^9/$_{16}$ in, while the rest sloped down to the throatplate where there was a final flat section of 5 in. At this point the foundation ring was some 2 ft 6^1/$_4$ in lower than the barrel at its joint with the throatplate. The copper and steel backplates were flanged and riveted together at the firehole and sloped forward. Above the crown the backplate was level. Both the firebox crown and the roof sloped from the throatplate at 1:21.841 to the backplate, the maximum height of the boiler being 3 ft 5 in above the centre line and the back corners 2 ft 10 in above the centre line. A sand gun was fitted as standard.

The firebox crown and the water spaces were stayed with $^1/_2$ in steel stays, except in the areas of the greatest expansion, where $^5/_8$ in Monel metal stays were used. The stays were riveted except in the firebox, where they had threaded nuts fitted inside the firebox. To give longitudinal strength to the boiler, end to end stays were fitted from the tubeplate to the backplate, a distance of some 30 ft $6^5/_{16}$ in internally. Additional short stays were used at each end to connect the tubeplate with the first ring and the backplate to the second ring. There were also cross stays fitted above the firebox crown. The water space increased from $3^3/_4$ in at the foundation ring to 5 in at the backplate end of the firebox crown and $5^5/_{16}$ in below the combustion chamber. The firebox was fitted with LMS standard mud-doors, and with washout plugs for both inspection and cleaning purposes.

The smokebox was held to the boiler by an external steel ring rivetted to the parallel section of the boiler just forward of the tubeplate. The boiler was assembled with stiffening plates at the rings, fitted wtih mainframe supporting stays, was held by a steadying bracket at the throatplate and was restrained by a diaphragm plate at the back end.

All the 'Duchesses' were fitted with the same tube arrangement and no changes were ever found necessary. There were 129 firetubes of $2^3/_8$ in outside diameter and 11 standard wire gauge (swg), and 40 flue tubes of $5^1/_8$ in outside diameter and 7 swg. All the tubes were 19 ft 3 in long between the tubeplates. Free areas for the boiler were:

Through flue tubes	3.66 sq. ft
Through small tubes	3.23 sq. ft
Total free area	6.89 sq. ft

This is only 13.8 per cent of the grate area, which indicates how difficult it is to achieve high percentages within the British loading gauge.

The superheater consisted of a cast-iron header which fed 40 triple elements of 1 in outside diameter and 11 swg, providing 120 paths for the steam. The superheater was subsequently modified with later builds of the class, changes in the thickness of the tube walls altering the superheater heating surfaces. The heating surface was reduced from 856 sq. ft with 13 swg to 830 sq. ft with 11 swg, and finally 822 sq. ft with 10 swg. The tube diameters stayed constant at 1 in. The last two locomotives of the class, Nos 6256 *Sir William A. Stanier FRS* and 6257 *City of Salford*, were both fitted with a 979 sq. ft superheater. However, this did not last long and the standard triple element superheater was subsequently fitted.

At this stage it is worth explaining that the method used for defining the heating surface area of superheaters was standardized by the Association of Locomotive Engineers in 1914 and is specified using the internal diameter of the tubes for all calculations and to ignore the return bends and the connection to the superheater head, where they are outside the large tubes. This is because the heating effect of

No. 6220 *Coronation* having the boiler fitted to the frames at Crewe on 29 April 1937.

National Railway Museum, York

the gases in this area is considered to be minimal. Consequently with a change in swg or thickness of the tube wall, (where the lower the swg number, the thicker the tube wall), it can be readily seen that the heating surface area will change, because of the smaller internal diameter, given a constant outside diameter.

The boiler was designed to work at a maximum pressure of 250 lb per sq. in, with a minimum safety factor of 4.75 times the working pressure. Boiler construction was still considered an art at the time the 'Duchesses' were built, and it is known Stanier considered that Crewe boiler shop was generally very good. The craftsmanship in the pattern and boiler shops was of a high standard, with the 'limits and fits' worked to a very high quality.

The regulator was the standard LMS type, with both pilot and main valves, and was controlled by a rod fitted internally to the boiler which passed through a stuffing box at the backplate. The boiler dome was fitted with baffle plates to stop water passing to the main steampipe, which was of 7 in diameter.

The firebox grate was built in three sections, the rear being level and the other sections sloping in line with the firebox shape, as already described. Nos 6220–8 were fitted with this arrangement but on No. 6229 *Duchess of Hamilton* the front part of the grate was built in two sections, consisting of two cast-iron frames which held cast-iron door sections. These could be opened simultaneously from the footplate. They were designed to assist in fire-dropping but they were not drop-grates in the accepted sense. Difficulties with efficient servicing of the firebox on the earlier locomotives led to these changes. A full drop-grate was introduced to the class after the Second World War and initially fitted to Nos 6253–7, whose boilers were built with this change from new. The rest of the class was fitted wtih the drop-grate design as boiler changes occurred.

The ashpan was effectively built in two sections, having to be divided to clear the trailing truck axle, and consequently at this point the ashpan was very shallow. A footplate control operated each of the two damper doors, which were fitted at either end of the ashpan, and this control was later modified to a more positive screw link. From No. 6225 *Duchess of Gloucester* onwards, ashpans were fitted with hopper doors in the two sections. The 'Duchesses' were not fitted with side doors on the ashpans until the last two were built in 1947–8, as these doors would have been inaccessible under the streamlined and cabside casing. Nos 6253–7 were fitted wtih self-emptying ashpans from new.

The safety valves were mounted on top of the combined wide/Belpaire firebox close to the backplate, and were the 2½ in pop-type valves set at 250 lb per sq. in. Due to the loading gauge the valves could not be set any further forward. The whistle was positioned horizontally, forward of the safety valves.

In the smokebox, the steampipes were placed well to the sides so as to make the bottom as clear as possible for ash and char removal. The junction for the inside and outside cylinders was on the outside of the smokebox, covered with the bulbous cover which can be so clearly seen on the nonstreamlined members of the class, prior to being fitted with smoke deflectors.

No. 46243 *City of Lancaster* at Crewe in 1952, still fitted with the sloping smokebox which wasn't removed until November 1958. She is seen here in BR blue livery.

Rex Conway

The smokebox curved down at the front to suit the casing on the streamlined versions, but as the casings were removed, and at subsequent major servicing, the smokeboxes were changed to match the fully rounded nonstreamlined smokeboxes. Even so, it took until May 1960 for No. 46246 *City of Manchester* to be the last to be fitted with the fully rounded smokebox. Later evidence would suggest that the change was more cosmetic than actual, with the curved bevel having a welded cover fitted to complete the shape of the nonstreamlined version of the smokebox. The preserved No. 46229 *Duchess of Hamilton* was found to be constructed in this way when the boiler was lifted from the frames for maintenance (see Chapter Ten). The smokebox plates fitted to the class were constructed of copper bearing steel and Nos 6253–7 were fitted from new with self-cleaning smokeboxes.

Both the live and exhaust steam injectors delivered to the top-feed clacks where they discharged onto trays in the steam space, and thence passed through a further pair of pipes to below the level of the water. The trays were designed to allow any air to be separated from the feed, before being passed into the boiler. The injectors were located – live steam on the left-hand side and exhaust steam on the right-hand side – below the footplate.

The whole concept of the boiler design and attachments was to enable the greatest free flow and generation of steam, a major consideration for the reliability and provision of any long-distance service. The fact that this was achieved with a high level of success indicates the skills, ability and quality of leadership of Stanier and his team. Complete boiler information, type numbers, etc. can be found in the appendices.

The footplate layout was similar to that of the 'Princess Royals' and consequently had a large degree of standardization, including the fold-down wooden seats on both sides of the footplate for the driver and fireman, although it is doubtful about how much use the fireman would have made of this facility during any West Coast Main Line service. The forward-lookout windows on the streamlined locomotives were smaller than those on the nonstreamlined members of the class due to the smaller clearance between the cab front and the streamlined casing. When the casings were removed these smaller lookouts were left fitted to the cab but were ultimately enlarged to the same size, as fitted from new, as those on the nonstreamlined members of the class. Trickle sanding was no longer used on LMS locomotives when the 'Duchesses' were designed, and steam sanding was applied to the front of the leading and intermediate driving wheels and to the rear of the intermediate driving wheels only.

Speedometers of the Stones-Dueta type were fitted to Nos 6220–4 but subsequently the BTH speedometers were considered more suitable and all locomotives up to 1944 were thus fitted, with Nos 6220–4 having the original Stones-Dueta type replaced. In 1940 a workshop order was raised to remove all speedometers and consequently this shortsighted requirement meant all the 'Duchess' class were to be operated without any method of speed recording. Consideration was given to refitting the class in 1947, and as a result Nos 6256–7 were built with the fittings, including a modified drive gear and mounting for the Flaman units which had similar drive to the BTH units. However, it is unclear whether these were in fact fitted as all drawings showing this modification are undated or do not indicate which, if any, locomotive the design was intended to fit. It wasn't until the late fifties or early sixties that Smith Stone units were fitted.

The streamlined casing was formed on wooden jigs and fitted to the boiler over a lightweight framework which straddled the boiler and boiler cladding. The casing was worked with great care and needed a high degree of skill to meet the tolerance of the wooden jigs and patterns. The front end of the boiler was fitted with a stronger framework which included a horizontal extension of the platforms as far as the rounded nose end. Below this, the casing extended around the cylinders, with a further extension where it was shaped round the buffer shanks, between which was a plain opening for the drawhook. The outside cylinders produced a definite widening and the casing fitted over them. A small step was fitted below the drawhook from No. 6225 *Duchess of Gloucester* onwards. The upper part of the nose opened up to give access to the smokebox and the inside valves, while the lower panels along the side of the locomotive were fitted with opening hatches which gave access to the mechanical lubricators. The sandboxes were fitted with extension pipes and screw caps which were flush with

The smokebox streamlined cover was produced using a wooden pattern. This is a rear view of the pattern, seen at Crewe.

National Railway Museum, York

the casing. Interestingly, the nonstreamlined 'Duchesses' were fitted with the same design of sandboxes and lubricators, which goes some way to explaining the less than clean design of the running boards on these locomotives.

On streamlined members of the class from No. 6225 *Duchess of Gloucester* onwards, small louvres were fitted on the left-hand side of the casing looking towards the front, just forward of the cylinders. These were only on one side and were designed to allow air to the Automatic Train Control (ATC) air filter. ATC was authorized to be fitted to Nos 6227, 6230, 6231 and 6233 in June 1939, with all the class to be modified at convenient shop times. The ATC fitted was the HUDD system, which was on trial on the London Tilbury & Southend line, and consequently all streamlined locomotives were fitted with the louvres. In October 1939 a works orders was raised to remove ATC from the fitted locomotives and all future modifications were to be held in abeyance. All material was to be removed from the four locomotives and returned to the signal stores in the Old Works at Crewe. It wasn't until the late fifties and early sixties that the BR ATC system was eventually fitted.

All the 'Duchesses' were fitted with the standard Stanier-design six-wheel tenders, having a capacity of 10 tons of coal and 4,000 gallons of water, the

Typical 'Duchess' running plates, with a profusion of sandbox fillers and oil fillers. Note also the name-plate details.

Author's Collection

amounts being based on the policies agreed by the LMS Mechanical and Electrical Engineering Committee meeting of 27 April 1932. The meeting recorded that the capacities for general purpose use should be 3,500 gallons of water but for extended long-distance runs 4,000 gallons would be more appropriate, and if a greater capacity was required it would be more cost effective to increase the number of water troughs. In fact the West Coast Main Line was well provided with water troughs, eleven in all, a far greater number than on the LNER route to the North. Keeping to the standard tenders also allowed the 'Duchesses' to use the existing 70 ft turntables without incurring additional problems. Only one 5,000 gallon tender was ever fitted to a 'Duchess' prior to preservation. This was during the locomotive exchanges of 1948 when No. 46236 *City of Bradford* was fitted with a Ministry of Supply tender, No. 79294, because of the lack of water troughs between Waterloo and Exeter. The tender was used with the LMS lettering on the side, even though the locomotive had by now entered BR service and had been renumbered, and despite the fact that the LMS had never owned such a tender. A proposal had been put forward for an increased capacity tender to be fitted to Nos 6256 and 6257, but this was later abandoned and the revised standard tender fitted instead. The increased capacity tender was to have contained 5,000 gallons of water and 12 tons of coal, with eight wheels and an overall length of

'Duchess' tender side details, showing the curved tops to the large Stanier tender and the aesthetically pleasing tender frames.

Author's Collection

27 ft 5 in, an increase in length for the complete locomotive of approximately 2 ft 2 in. The tender had a similar but larger outline to that of the Ivatt Standard class locomotive tenders.

A Stanier experimental corridor tender existed but it is unknown whether this was ever used with a 'Duchess'. This tender was in traffic as late as 1952 during the comparative tests carried out by BR between the Austerity 2–8–0 No. 90464 and a 2–10–0. It is understood that the tests were carried out to evaluate the difference between the boiler types, i.e. narrow versus wide fireboxes. The BR Standard 9F 2–10–0 was being designed at Brighton at this time, so whether the data gained had any value is unknown. The tender was still painted crimson lake, had the LMS lettering on the side and was used with the black liveried test locomotives. The tender was designed for attachment to any locomotive and was used to test the water and coal consumption of locomotives under trials, having the bunker divided in two, half carrying 3 tons of loose coal for nontest use and the other half carrying 3 tons in 1 cwt bags. The water capacity was 3,500 gallons, which was fitted with metering between the tender and locomotive, and also fitted were ducts for carrying cables to the dynamometer car. This tender was converted to a standard 4,000 gallon version in 1959 and ran with 'Black 5' No. 45235.

Three main designs of tender were fitted to the 'Duchesses'. All were fitted with coal-pushers and can be classified as follows:

Type A   The original streamlined style, of welded tank construction and coupled to Nos 6220–9 and 6235–52.

Type B   The original nonstreamlined versions, of welded tank construction and coupled to Nos 6230–4.

Type C   Nonstreamlined versions of partly riveted tank construction and coupled to Nos 6253–6 and 46257. There were two slightly different configurations. On one the cutaway at the side tank front was high, as on Nos 6253–5, and on the other the cutaway began immediately above the handrail, as on Nos 6256 and 46257.

When the locomotives were de-streamlined, tenders which had similarly been destreamlined were easily recognized because they were missing the vertical handrails at the rear and the steps behind the rear wheels. Across the class, only sixteen locomotives retained the original fitted tenders and a further nine had only one change. Tender No. 9749 was the most travelled, having been coupled to no fewer than six different locomotives, and finally being coupled to No. 46246 *City of Manchester*. No. 6242 *City of Glasgow* was the locomotive with the most tender changes, six in all, which included four different tenders after the initial allocation.

Tender changes were nearly always like for like but sometimes there were oddities where streamlined locomotives ran with nonstreamlined tenders, or vice versa. Nonstreamlined locomotives Nos 6249–52, built during the Second World War, always ran with streamlined tenders, as these had already been built for them. The other mismatches which could be considered semi-permanent were Nos 6230–1, which ran from 1945 with ex-streamlined tenders, and No. 6223, which ran from 1946 with the nonstreamlined tender originally fitted to No. 6230. Further details of tender numbers and allocations can be found in the appendices.

The tenders were constructed with frames which had an equally divided wheelbase of 7 ft 6 in between the wheel centres; the wheels were 4 ft 3 in diameter. The tender was fitted with a single steam brake cylinder which applied brake blocks to the rear of the wheels simultaneously with the locomotive steam brake. The frames were 1 in plates outside the wheels, with extra strength being provided by a pair of $^5/_8$ in plates between the wheels which acted as stays between the front and rear dragboxes. The mainframes had lightening holes and were braced across the bottom by horizontal stays, by the dragboxes at each end and at the top by additional horizontal stays with vertical plates.

The drawgear from the locomotive to the tender consisted of a main drawbar on the centre line and two auxiliary drawbars, one to each side. The intermediate buffers were 3 ft 8 in apart with coil springs behind the dragbox. The rear of the tender was fitted with standard buffers and drawgear.

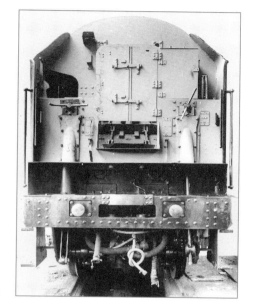

Fireman's view of the 'Duchess' tender, showing the water scope hand wheel and tender hand brake. Also shown are the coal doors and coal shovelling plate; note the details of the coal-pusher. (Compare this with the photograph on p. 73.)
National Railway Museum, York

The tenders were fitted with the LMS-style water scoop, complete with deflector plates at the front to help channel water into the scoop. The water passed via a cast-iron trunk into the tank. The scoop was operated by a handle mounted on the faceplate of the tender and was connected by bevel gear. Normally the scoop was hinged up. This design originated because the longer trailing length of the 'Duchesses', causing a greater throw-over, which made the original LMS design impractical. Operation of the device required a fine degree of judgment on behalf of the fireman, particularly when travelling at speed with a critical driver and a front coach full of important passengers. It was not unknown to raise the scoop just a little too late, causing an overflow from the tank and giving the passengers in the front coaches an unexpected bath. Staff on the West Coast Main Line expresses were well known for closing windows on the front coach at such times to protect the passengers. Interestingly, the railway companies also seemed to expect excessive overflows, in that the ballast around the troughs was protected by timbers placed alongside the sleepers to stop the overflow washing the ballast away.

On the West Coast Main Line it was also possible for a locomotive to miss topping up the tanks because of a preceding train, something that happened particularly with high-speed services like the 'Coronation Scot' when catching up with slower freight or long-distance stopping trains. Examples of 'Duchesses' having to stop at water towers, having missed topping up the tank at earlier troughs, are not unusual. The problem was that the troughs took a finite time to fill after being used and this could be longer than the separation time between trains. In 1949 the

No. 46253 *City of St Albans* hauling the 11.10 service from Birmingham to Carlisle, seen here at the Moor troughs on 8 August 1959.

M.H. Walshaw, Hugh Davis Collection

refill time had been reduced to 2 minutes after a rebuild of the troughs and the feed tanks, although this was known to be too slow for some services. Typically, up to a hundred trains could take water on a normal winter's day.

The troughs on the 'Coronation Scot' route were on average 500 to 700 yd long and had a capacity of between 2,500 and 3,500 gallons. A locomotive was able to lift approximately 2,000 gallons, although a figure of 3,000 gallons has been recorded. However, a figure this high was unusual on the 'Coronation Scot' because of the speed with which it passed over the troughs. It has been suggested by footplate crew that the optimum speed was approximately 50 m.p.h. for the least wastage through spray.

On the tender, access to the coal space was via a folding door which was normally kept closed, as the coal would be removed from the gap at the bottom edge between the doors and the bunker floor. This floor was extended slightly at this point to give a shovelling plate. On the fireman's side of the tender, a long tunnel was provided, to stow the fire irons, etc. and on the driver's side was a wood-lined compartment in which the crew could store foodboxes and clothing.

The coal-pusher consisted of a $10\frac{1}{2}$ in steam-powered piston which was fitted to the sloping floor of the bunker. This pushed two wedge-shaped rams down the slope. The piston was powered from steam derived and fed from the manifold on the firebox via a flexible connection to the operating control. This was fitted inside the fire iron tunnel. The exhaust for the coal-pusher escaped from the protective plate which covered the piston at the rear of the bunker. This was a

A 'Duchess' coal-pusher, looking towards the rear of the tender. Note the steam cylinder and sloping coal space.

Author's Collection

piece of machinery that was never totally successful, which was probably because of the desire to keep it simple, when in fact what was needed was a complicated movement. Originally the exhaust was passed into the water tank to impart some extra preheating effects, but this was found to cause additional aeration in the water feed to the boiler and was subsequently modified.

The tenders for the streamlined locomotives were fitted with two doors on the sideplate extensions adjacent to the water-filler lids, of which there were also two. The doors slide back to give access for the water hoses to the tanks and were accessible via a ladder on the rear of the tender. The nonstreamlined tenders had the standard centre tank lid, with bracket steps behind the rear wheels for access, although vertical handrails were fitted.

In addition, the streamlined tenders were fitted with a cowl which aligned with the locomotive roof and was designed to minimize draughts on the footplate. This was not just for the footplate crew's comfort but was also to stop the dust storm created by coal dust from the bunker blinding the crew. The first five streamlined locomotives were not originally fitted with this cowl, but had it fitted later. The streamlined tenders were also fitted with a shrouding which partially covered the springs and wheels. In addition, the rear body sides were extended to line up with the buffer faces so as to decrease the gap between the first coach and the tender. This was designed to help reduce wind resistance and the frontal resistance of the first coach. Clearly, the nonstreamlined locomotives were not designed to be fitted with this type of tender and when the 'Duchess' streamlining was finally discarded, the cowls, side extensions and shrouding were removed so that from an initial view there were few differences between the original streamlined and nonstreamlined tenders.

During Ivatt's reign as the last CME of the LMS, modifications to the 'Duchesses' were carried out to increase the mileage between maintenance and shopping. These included self-cleaning smokeboxes, rocking grates, a redesigned rear truck, and Sefco and Timken bearings fitted to all boxes. The changes are discussed in full in Chapter Seven.

The 'Duchesses' carried a number of liveries during the lifetime of the class. In fact, there were eleven different paint schemes, including two experimental schemes. All of the locomotives were painted British Rail green at one stage, during the two years between August 1955 and December 1957. Initially, the first five members of the class were painted in blue with four silver bands along the body, forming chevrons across the front of the locomotive, just above the drawhook. The outer two of the four stripes were thicker than the inner two and gave a very strong impression of speed and power. All four bands were lined with a darker blue band, the wheels were dark blue and the motion and tyres were brightly polished. The name-plates had a blue background with silver letters and rims.

The next streamlined locomotives to be built were painted in crimson lake livery with gold bands. The bands were lined with black, and had a very thin vermilion line between the gold and the black. The name-plates on these locomotives again had silver lettering with silver rims but this time with a crimson lake background. The wheels were painted black. Interestingly, when *Duchess of Hamilton* went to the USA as *Coronation*, she was left in crimson lake livery, which left *Coronation*, alias *Duchess of Hamilton*, in blue, a livery which No. 6229 had never worn.

The five prewar nonstreamlined 'Duchesses', Nos 6230–4, were completed in LMS standard crimson lake, having gold lining edged with vermilion. Strictly speaking, this was also nonstandard, as the LMS colour scheme was for straw edging to the gold lining, although the difference between the two probably went unnoticed among the travelling public.

From then on the class progressed through wartime black, LMS black, BR black, and the BR colours of blue, green and red. A full listing of the various colour schemes applied to all the members of the class can be found in the appendices. When the locomotives were painted in final BR red, the smokebox and the smoke deflectors were all painted black, though there is some evidence to suggest that during 1963, No. 46225 *Duchess of Gloucester* may have run with the smoke deflectors painted red, even though the smokebox was black. The details are very sketchy and any additional information would be useful.

Two experimental colour schemes were applied to members of the class. No. 6234 *Duchess of Abercorn* was painted in what the LMS called grey in 1946, which was similar to the Royal Air Force blue. The lining was gold with crimson edging, similar to the original Ivatt style, and there was no boiler lining. It is

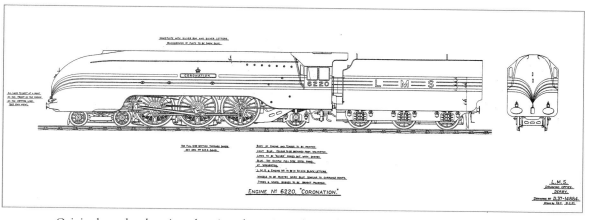

Original works drawing showing the paint scheme for No. 6220 *Coronation*. Note the absence of the shroud from the rear of the footplate roof to the tender, the single chimney and the original scheme for the speedometer drive.

National Railway Museum, York

understood that the lining was only applied to the right-hand side of the locomotive. The name-plates had a Midland red background and the 'LMS' on the tender was closely spaced. Seven members of the class were painted in an experimental blue livery which was somewhat darker than that which was applied in 1950 to nearly all of the class, before the application of BR green started the following year. Included in that change was *Duchess of Abercorn*, which went from experimental grey to experimental blue within two years.

In 1964, a broad, yellow, diagonal stripe was added to the side of the cabs of the remaining members of the class. This stripe was only broken by the locomotive numbers. The stripe was to warn crew and others that the 'Duchesses' were not allowed south of Crewe because the size of the engines fouled the new standard clearances for the high-voltage catenary. Additionally, high-voltage warning plates were positioned around the locomotive to warn crew when climbing on or around the locomotive.

Nos 6236, 6256 and 46257 ran with 'BRITISH RAILWAYS' on the tender, and the rest of the class had either or both of the BR lion and wheel symbols on the tender sides, at any one time, during the lifetime of the class.

One interesting slant on the liveries was the practice of the LMS to take official photographs of each member of the class at the time of completion. Presumably for logistical reasons and also for convenience, a number of photographs illustrating the City members of the class were taken at the same time, using one locomotive suitably renumbered and renamed, to represent each city. Unfortunately the effect was to have the wrong numbers and names combined and even streamlined versions that were not! This was due to the change in the numbers and names at a later date, caused by the renaming of No. 6244 as *King*

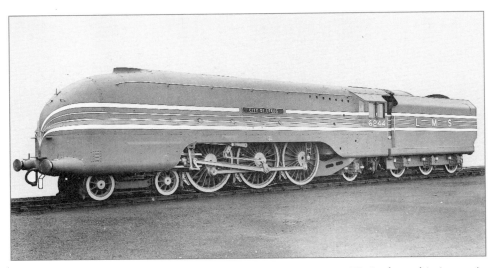

No. 6244 *City of Leeds* prior to being named *King George VI*. In fact, this is poetic licence, as this photograph was taken in July 1939, some twelve months before *City of Leeds* was built! This locomotive was in fact No. 6235 *City of Birmingham*. The real No. 6244 was renamed in June 1941.

National Railway Museum, York

George VI in April 1941, having originally been *City of Leeds*. Subsequently No. 6248 became the 'real' *City of Leeds*, which moved all later names. Typically, photographs exist of *City of Nottingham* as a streamlined locomotive, No. 6250, neither of which were correct! This would have been the correct number if the naming order had stayed as planned, but No. 6250 was never to be streamlined. Original selected names are shown in the appendices. In addition, No. 6229 *Duchess of Hamilton* was built out of sequence, being completed after No. 6234 *Duchess of Abercorn*, presumably because the latter was the last of a batch of nonstreamlined locomotives and No. 6229 was streamlined.

With the announcement of the new Pacific design, it was hoped by both the travelling public and the enthusiasts that the success of the 'Princess Royal' class could be improved upon with the new west coast services to Scotland. In fact, when the timings were announced there was general disappointment in that a 6½ hour service to Glasgow was planned, with one stop at Carlisle. The service was to commence on 5 July 1937 and was to be named the 'Coronation Scot'.

The LMS came in for some criticism when the timings were announced, but some salient facts need to be stated before considering whether the criticism was justified. Unlike the LNER, the gradient profile for the West Coast Main Line was, to say the least, difficult, particularly bearing in mind Shap and Beattock. In addition, the scheduled timings over the Caledonian section of the route were faster than any previous service. It also has to be remembered that while publicity

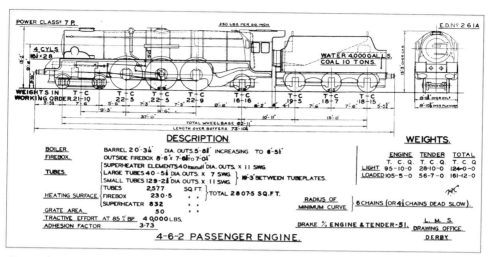

General arrangement of nonstreamlined 'Duchess', complete with double chimney, complete running plates over the front of the cylinders and no smoke deflectors.

National Railway Museum, York

is the life blood of any company, that company has to make money and this is gained by reliability. Thus, it is better to run a service which consistently meets timings, under all conditions and with maximum loadings, than to attempt to reproduce a performance gained under perfect conditions, at all times.

There has been some recent criticism of the 'Duchesses', when compared with the Gresley A4s, particularly with regard to timings, reliability and longevity. The issue of longevity will be dealt with elsewhere, but with regard to timings and reliability, I believe it is unfortunate that critical comments based on limited interpretation of statistics should attempt to increase the competitive temperature between the two London and Scotland express routes, particularly when it is known that the CMEs of the two rival companies had nothing but the greatest respect for each other and their individual designs of locomotive. In fact, Sir Nigel Gresley is known to have commented that the 'Coronation Scot' required a higher power output than the 'Silver Jubilee' expresses of the LNER because of the heavier tare loads. The point remains that the 'Duchesses' ran the west coast services with loads of up to 600 tons, reliably and with panache. But before leaving this vexed situation, it is worth mentioning that even when using figures supplied by the critics, the reliability of the 'Coronation Scot' to Glasgow was stated as being on time or early 100 per cent of the time during September 1937, while the LNER 'Coronation' service was only 77 per cent on time or early, and that was while carrying only 62 per cent of the maximum passenger load.

As part of the improvement in the service, timings notwithstanding, the track between London and Glasgow was realigned so as to cope with the higher speeds.

Modifications were made to some fifty areas where speed had been restricted. By and large the system was remodelled to allow speeds of up to 90 m.p.h. on curves, with a minimum of 75 m.p.h. In addition, junctions were modified to enable faster main-line traffic and the loading gauge restrictions were upgraded as much as possible. Where the loading gauge was changed this was as much due to Stanier's personality as it was to the agreement of the civil engineer. At that time the civil engineer was the only officer on the railway who had absolute authority to stop trains for breaching the 'Civils' requirements. By quoting engineering facts and through the force of his personality Stanier was able to persuade the civil engineer that his Pacific designs were compliant. Having said that, with the advent of E.F. Trench as civil engineer the overall regime was much more relaxed and amenable to change. One area that was not changed, however, and in fact was not to be changed for some fifty years after the 'Duchesses', was the 20 m.p.h. speed restriction at Crewe.

Much has been written about the press run to Crewe using No. 6220 *Coronation* on 29 June 1937, in particular about the differences between the locomotive speedometer recorded speed and the observers' records on the train, and whether the LNER speed record of 113 m.p.h. was broken on this run, but what is not in dispute is the high-speed approach to Crewe station when the train negotiated the 20 m.p.h. restricted reverse curve at approximately 50 m.p.h. with no noticeable effect on the engine and little damage to the track itself. This has to be indicative of the extremely good ride and surefootedness of the 'Duchesses', as well as the wisdom of Stanier's insistence on the accuracy of tolerance for the leading bogie and trailing truck. One wonders whose head would have rolled if the locomotive had been derailed.

A comment from R.A. Riddles, Stanier's personal assistant, who was riding on the footplate at the time, is worth recording.

> The signals for platform number 3 at Crewe, entered by a reversed curve with a 20 m.p.h. speed restriction, came into sight. We were still doing 60 to 70 m.p.h. when we spotted the platform signal. The crockery of the dining car crashed. Down we came to 52 m.p.h. through the curve. With the engine riding like the great lady she is there wasn't a thing we could do about it but hold on and let her take it. And take it she did; past a sea of pallid faces on the platform we ground to a dead stand, safe and sound and still on the rails.

It is incredible to consider that the train had passed over in succession, three reverse curves in the crossovers and six entry and exit curves, the first being entered at an estimated speed of 57 m.p.h.! Little wonder that pallid faces met the arrival of the train. The last $10\frac{1}{2}$ miles from passing Whitmore to a dead stand at Crewe were achieved in 6 minutes 58 seconds!

The return trip from Crewe back to London was one of the fastest ever recorded in Great Britain. The 158 miles to Euston were covered in 119 minutes at an average speed of 79.7 m.p.h., something that compares very favourably with today's modern electric services. On both the Down and Up journeys, *Coronation* was crewed by Driver T.J. Clarke and Fireman J. Lewis, both of Crewe.

A postscript to the event was the comment made by the LMS vice-president, Sir Ernest Lemon, when he addressed the guests at the press lunch. Speaking about the sudden and violent entry into Crewe, he said, 'Of course gentlemen, you realize that we shan't need to do this kind of thing on every trip of the 'Coronation Scot'; we were coming in a little faster than we shall have to, in the ordinary course.'

There have been many comments made about the value of streamlining, and certainly publicity was a major factor, as was the influence of Stamp, but as always there is the question of maintenance costs and time consumed during that maintenance for removal of the streamlined covers. Certainly, after the Second World War the disadvantages were clear, when all the streamlined examples were 'defrocked'.

Interestingly, five 'Duchesses' were built during 1938 in the nonstreamlined design. Information is sparse on why this decision was taken but one has to assume that even then maintenance costs were becoming more of an issue. This, coupled with the desire to have a locomotive with the same presence but without the inappropriateness of streamlining on anything other than 'Coronation Scot' services, must have been a big motivator, but why then return to streamlined versions, particularly during the war? One has to assume that Lord Stamp and the publicity department had a strong say in the matter.

CHAPTER FIVE

PERFORMANCE AND THE STREAMLINED ERA

The performance of the 'Duchesses' produced some exceptional results, delivering large amounts of power over extended runs. In addition, the ability to provide that bit extra on every-day services enabled crews to deal with the changing conditions of the long West Coast Main Line. The performance criteria for the 'Duchesses' were expressed in the power rating of the locomotives. The classification was 7P during the LMS period. This was expressed as 10,080–11,200 lb at 50 m.p.h. and was the theoretical force at the wheel rims when new, ignoring any internal resistance. Subsequently, during British Railways times the 'Duchesses' were reclassified as power class 8P. Although the locomotives' power output did not change, the difference in classification was a result of BR's change in power calculations.

The timetable set the number of trains to be run and in consequence the number of diagrams that each locomotive was to operate. Thus the crew numbers, loads and class of locomotive required were determined. Clearly, within all this scheduling there had to be an allowance for maintenance and repairs, either at the home shed, or the works for major repairs. Generally, British practice was for an availability of 85 per cent, a figure that was never attainable by any large passenger locomotives, for which 75 per cent was considered good. Less than the required availability was caused by various factors and the information was gathered from the returns submitted by each individual shed. The working days for all locomotives were accounted for and the status of each locomotive given, i.e. in use, available but not used, in for examination or repairs, awaiting material or a decision on works repairs, or in works. Sunday was not included in availability records but was included in terms of annual mileage and consumables. Below are the average annual mileages and percentage availability of the four major British Railways regions' express locomotives in 1950, 1954 and 1957. No doubt the aficionados of the Gresley A4 Pacifics will be disappointed to see that the 'Duchesses' were able to deliver both a higher annual mileage and a better availability for these periods. While mileages of the 'King' and 'Merchant Navy' classes is significantly less than the 'Duchesses' this is because of the shorter runs available on the Southern and Western Regions.

No. 46244 *King George VI* with the 07.45 Glasgow to Euston express service, 'The Caledonian', passing Apsley with a fairly light load of eight trailing bogies in 1957. This view clearly shows the massive proportions of the boiler on these locomotives. Note the cylinder for the coal-pusher on the top of the tender and also the lack of coal.

National Railway Museum, York

Class		Power class	1950 miles	%	1954 miles	%	1957 miles	%
'Duchess'	4–6–2	8P	69,649	70	74,333	72	74,144	72
A4	4–6–2	8P	54,641	69	62,841	70	65,575	72
'Merchant Navy'	4–6–2	8P	45,833	56	46,128	57	58,575	64
'King'	4–6–0	8P	55,978	61	51,010	56	50,328	55

Mileage is average annual mileage per locomotive.

The servicing schedules for passenger locomotives were complex and involved, being based both on mileage and days in steam. Obviously these would have to be matched to keep the down times to a minimum. This caused difficulties as the mileage was used as a measure of the wear and tear of the moving parts and was not necessarily related to time in steam, bearing in mind the hours a boiler will be in steam between turns or during lighting up, generation of steam and cooling-down periods.

No. 46245 *City of London* at Willesden, then its home shed, on a misty 26 January 1964.
John Wickham

Every passenger locomotive had to have a daily inspection and each week the major express locomotives had to stop for a Boiler Full Examination (BFX), which could take up to eight days. The BFX was an examination of a locomotive in steam, and a check of the ancillary items like cylinder cocks, sanding gear, self-cleaning smokebox, rocking grate and ashpan hopper, to make sure that all were working correctly. In addition, the tubes were checked for any obstructions.

The boiler was cooled for the examination of the firebox and this was accomplished by passing cold water through the boiler at a prescribed rate so as to slowly displace the hot water. The rate of change was at 5 gallons per minute for 2 hours, 12 gallons per minute for another 2 hours and a final 25 gallons per minute for 30 minutes.

Every 14–16 days the boiler was washed out and this required the boiler to be cooled as for the BFX examination, except that the final 25 gallons per minute was used for an additional 90 minutes till the boiler was absolutely cold. The boiler had to be cold because the LMS used cold water for the boiler wash out. To enable this task to be completed the wash-out plugs and mud-hole doors were removed. The firebox water spaces, firebox crown and the boiler barrel were cleaned out using a high-pressure water jet. A boiler smith would then carry out a complete examination of the boiler. With the cooling periods, the lighting-up times and the time for the service itself it can be seen that protracted periods occurred when locomotives were unavailable for traffic.

Waiting to work south from Carlisle on 28 December 1963 are, left, No. 46237 *City of Bristol* with the Up 'Royal Scot' and, right, *City of Coventry* with the 10.10 relief to Birmingham from Edinburgh.

John Wickham

In addition, many nonmoving parts had to have regular examinations at 3–5 week intervals. In particular, water gauge frame cocks and passages were checked for clearance, with new gauge glasses fitted. The brakes were tested, which included testing the quality of the ejector operation, and the train steam-heating and reducing valves were tested with any defective hoses replaced. At 7–9 weeks the firebox fusible plugs were replaced and the clacks, injectors and driver's brake valve checked. The safety valves were checked at 9–15 weeks to make sure they operated at between 245 lb per sq. in and 255 lb per sq. in.

The moving parts examination started at 5,000–6,000 miles, although for the 'Duchesses' only the wheels, tyres and tender tanks were checked this frequently. The motion was examined and partially dismantled at 10,000–12,000 miles, with crank axles, bogies, drawgear, axlebox pads and lubrication checked. In addition, the piston rings were changed. The piston valve rings were changed at 20,000–24,000 miles. Finally, at 30,000–36,000 miles the tender and the locomotive had to be separated for the examination of the intermediate drawgear and rubbing plates. Additionally, the pistons and piston valves were withdrawn and checked, steam and exhaust ports cleaned, all the smokebox fittings checked and the crankpins examined. For all the LMS Pacifics the motion and valve gear was returned to Crewe for this examination. Consequently, all 'Duchesses', regardless of their home shed, went to Crewe North shed for this service.

The elapsed time for the completion of these examinations was cumulative, as the 10,000 mile examinations would include the work for the 5,000 mile examination as well. It was always the optimistic wish that all examinations should not exceed 24 hours in the sheds, except for boiler repairs. This was probably manageable for the lesser examinations but the more extensive the work became the more chance there was of defective or damaged components being discovered. In addition, nonsafety-related or noncritical defects were held over till the next examination period, which increased the Down time, although availability would have fallen to seriously low figures if minor or noncritical repairs had been carried out at the time of each incident.

It was possible to rectify many problems at the locomotive's home shed but some jobs presented particular difficulties or aggravation, typically turning the bogies on the 'Duchesses' to even up the tyre wear. This involved heavy lifting at the shed, so consequently the practice developed of leaving the bogie frames *in situ*, dropping each wheel set and changing them over.

In addition to the shed examinations were the periods when the locomotives were taken out of service for major overhauls, which took place at Crewe works. The 'Duchesses' went into the shops every eight months, and unless passed as suitable for a further short period of operation were passed to Crewe for either a heavy or light repair. The repair classification depended on the type of work to be carried out:

1. Boiler change   Heavy
2. Combination of new tyres, or new cylinders or boiler retubed,
   or motion or brake gear overhauled   Heavy
3. One of 2. and a variety of other small repairs   Light

The repairs would also be classified as Intermediate or General. The difference between the two was that normally the boiler remained in place for an Intermediate repair, although other work could make it a Heavy Intermediate. Further, the interval between General and Intermediate repairs, despite the nominal eight months, was not equal. This was because the items not requiring attention at the Intermediate stage dictated the timescales before the next shop repair. This was particularly true of the boiler. Thus it can be seen that with major passenger locomotives like the 'Duchesses' the greater the mileage the more frequent the stops for examination or workshop repairs. Hence, the availability figures compared with the mileage give a very good indication of the quality of the 'Duchesses' as a whole.

Of the many logged runs carried out by the 'Duchesses', arguably the most famous is the record-breaking press run to Crewe with the 'Coronation Scot' hauled by No. 6220 *Coronation*, when a speed of 114 m.p.h. was recorded. In his book *British Pacific Locomotives*, C.J. Allan, who was timing the journey from within the train, suggests that the actual timed speed was 113 m.p.h. The official speed was taken from the locomotive speed indicator, not the most accurate instrument, while Allan, D.S.M. Barrie and S.P.W. Corbett were recording the time against distance. In any case it is agreed that given more distance a speed of over 115 m.p.h. could have been readily achieved.

No. 46255 *City of Hereford* working the 10.30 Euston to Liverpool Lime Street service passing Woodside sidings on 19 October 1958.

M.H. Walshaw, Hugh Davis Collection

Not to be dissuaded by the results of the Down journey, the operating department had scheduled an equally fast run on the return to Euston, a time of 135 minutes being allowed, with Driver Clarke being given a free hand regarding timings. The run was one of the fastest recorded in Great Britain. The schedule was cut by 16 minutes, with the 158 miles from Crewe to Euston taking exactly 119 minutes, an average of 79.7 m.p.h. throughout the whole journey. The 150.1 miles from Betley Road to Kilburn were completed at an average speed of 83.2 m.p.h., while the 72.15 miles from Welton to Kilburn were completed at an average speed of 88.9 m.p.h. A speed of 100 m.p.h. was reached at Castlethorpe, north of Wolverton, and 99 m.p.h. achieved at King's Langley, and speeds of 93–95 m.p.h. were logged at other points on the route. This was a great run and gave ample evidence of the power and ability of the 'Duchesses'. Further details of both the Up and Down runs are in the table below.

LMS EUSTON-CREWE, 'CORONATION SCOT' 29 JUNE 1937
LOCOMOTIVE NO. 6220 *CORONATION*
Load: 8 coaches, 263 tons tare, 270 tons gross

Down Journey					Up Journey			
Distance miles	*Scheduled mins*	*Actual mins*	*Speed m.p.h.*		*Distance miles*	*Scheduled mins*	*Actual mins*	*Speed m.p.h.*
0.0	0	0.00	0	Euston	158.0	135	119.00	–
5.4	8	7.53	68	Willesden Junction	152.6	127	112.50	85
17.45	18	17.02	86.5	Watford Junction	140.55	117.5	104.53	84
31.65	30	27.45	80.5	Tring	126.35	107	95.23	86.5
46.65	41	38.57	82	Bletchley	111.35	93	85.10	89

Down Journey					Up Journey			
Distance miles	Schedule mins	Actual mins	Speed m.p.h.			Distance miles	Schedule mins	Actual mins	Speed m.p.h.
62.85	53.5	51.09	86	Blisworth		95.15	82	74.42	92
82.55	70	66.28	39	Rugby		75.45	66	59.27	40
97.10	82	79.05	83	Nuneaton		60.90	54	43.29	90
110.0	94	89.24	77	Tamworth		48.0	42	38.55	90
116.25	99	94.25	76.5	Lichfield		41.75	37	34.44	92
133.55	115	109.56	30	Stafford		24.45	23	20.58	30
158.0	135	129.46	–	Crewe		0.0	0	0.00	0

Speed was reduced at Stafford and Rugby for the curves.

The 'Coronation Scot' was booked to cover the 299.1 miles to Carlisle in 283 minutes and to continue over the 102.3 miles to Glasgow in 105 minutes. A single engine worked the complete route and a tare weight of 297 tons was scheduled. The performance of No. 6220 *Coronation* was examined during normal operational service by the addition of the dynamometer car. At the time of the test the locomotive had run just under 30,000 miles since the last heavy repair and 220 miles since the last piston and valve examination, and consequently was in excellent condition. Overall coal consumption for the single trip was approximately 7 tons, which was a comfortable margin for this size of train. A summary of the results of the dynamometer trials is shown below:

EUSTON TO GLASGOW AND RETURN

402 miles in each direction		
Weight of train (tons tare)		331
Average running speed (m.p.h.)		60.4
Coal consumption	lb per mile	39.2
	lb per dhp hr	3.03
	lb per sq. ft of grate area per hr	47.3
Water consumption	galls per mile	32.3
	lb per dhp hr	25.0
Evaporation	lb of water per lb of coal	8.24
Average dhp		825

Although the concept of the 'Duchesses' was operation of the high-speed services on the West Coast Main Line, their versatility enabled them to haul heavy loads and to operate named express services across the LMS system. Examples of sharp timings with heavy loadings include the Down 'Merseyside Express' in the autumn of 1938, hauled by No. 6229 *Duchess of Hamilton*. With a load of 488 tons, 520 tons gross, the 189.6 miles were covered in a net time of 188 minutes, an average of 60.6 m.p.h. over the total run. No. 6228 *Duchess of Rutland* also gave an excellent account of herself on the Carlisle to Euston 16.00 Saturday service, also in the autumn of 1938, arriving at Euston 7½ minutes early despite a 6 minute late start at Carlisle, regained over Shap, a 9 minute delay in departure

No. 46236 *City of Bradford* on the 08.38 service from Carlisle to Euston, seen here at the Moor troughs on 8 August 1959.

M.H. Walshaw, Hugh Davis Collection

from Crewe, and a further 10 minute delay on route, including two dead stands for signals. The train was 490 tons gross and the overall net time for the 158.1 miles was 151½ minutes.

While these runs and many more like them indicated that a very successful locomotive had been designed which was proving to be very free running, the maximum haulage capacity had yet to be ascertained. Any doubts about the capability of the 'Duchesses' were to be dispelled when on Sunday 26 February 1939, No. 6234 *Duchess of Abercorn* hauled a special train of 604 tons tare, including a dynamometer car, between Crewe and Glasgow and return. *Duchess of Abercorn* was fitted with the double blastpipe and chimney and, as has already been noted, a previous run over the same route with the same locomotive prior to the fitting of the modified chimney arrangement, produced a very indifferent performance. On that occasion it had been impossible to keep to time or maintain full steam pressure.

The reason for the trial was not to test the locomotive in normal service but to push its capabilities to the limits on loading. The trial consisted of a total of 487 miles on a double home trip. No more than 2 hours were allowed for the turn round and no special attention was given to the fire. The train consisted of twenty coaches, including the dynamometer car, with no banking assistance being given over either Beattock or Shap. The finest effort was made on the Up journey, when hauling over twice the load of the 'Coronation Scot' the time between Glasgow and Carlisle was only 1½ minutes more than the schedule for that train.

To give some idea of the performance, *Duchess of Abercorn* had to lift the 604 tons tare unassisted from almost sea level at Carnforth to 914 ft above sea level at

Shap in just over 31 miles, and again by 1,000 ft from Carlisle to Beattock Summit in just under 50 miles. At Shap the ascent was made at an average speed of 56.5 m.p.h. and at Beattock at 53.2 m.p.h., and both summits were cleared at approximately 30 m.p.h. On the Up journey the climb from Motherwell to Beattock Summit, just under 40 miles, was taken at 62 m.p.h., a very creditable performance even when compared to today's electric traction. Crossing Beattock at a mile a minute was a very special event with that amount of trailing load.

It was during this run that the greatest drawbar pull ever recorded by a revenue-earning steam locomotive occurred. A reading of 2,282 hp, the equivalent of a calculated indicated horsepower of 3,333 hp, was recorded. Drawbar horsepower in the range 1,800–2,000 was maintained over a considerable distance and coal consumption averaged 68.7 lb per mile, with 3.12 lb per dhp per hr, a figure comparable with normal every-day performance. The footplate crews for these epic trips were: Crewe to Carlisle, Driver G. Garrett and Fireman S. Farrington; Carlisle to Glasgow, Driver J. Marshall and Fireman D. Lynn; and on the return run, Glasgow to Carlisle, Driver N. Mclean and Fireman A. Smith; and Carlisle to Crewe, Driver Garrett and Fireman Farrington took over again. Full details of the run can be seen below. At the time, some comments were made that the results were the exception rather than the norm, but as we will see, the power and performances were repeated a number of times throughout the life of the class.

	CREWE TO GLASGOW						GLASGOW TO CREWE					
	Carnforth–Shap Summit			Gretna–Beattock Summit			Motherwell–Beattock Summit			Carlisle–Shap Summit		
Ascent (miles)	12.96	13.08	5.69	17.27	13.96	10.13	5.42	6.74	17.28	13.03	4.77	13.68
Average dhp	1,870	1,668	1,830	1,598	1,609	1,724	1,923	1,520	1,860	1,822	2,000	1,560
Max. dhp	2,120	1,934	2,065	1,733	1,823	2,081	1,998	1,638	2,282	2,511	2,394	2,331
Max. ihp (calc.)	3,209	2,806	2,963	2,236	2,556	2,761	2,583	2,138	3,333	3,248	3,241	3,021
Average speed	68	53	47.9	59.3	72.5	36.8	46.7	46.1	63.4	43.9	71.4	44.4
Cut-off	20	25	25	20	20	30	20	20	30	30	20	30
% of stroke	25	25	35	25	25	40	30	25	35	35	30	40
Boiler pressure (psi)	250	245	240	250	245	245	250	245	245	245	230	245

It is understood that the operating department considered that one of the purposes of the trial with *Duchess of Abercorn* was to test the feasibility of combining services as much as possible and consequently increasing the trailing loads. This was particularly true of the trains north of Crewe. Interestingly, however successful the trial was, no subsequent attempt was made to replicate the

No. 6220 *Coronation* (also known as No. 6229 *Duchess of Hamilton*) secured in the hold of SS *Belpamela*, with Club Car 823 to the left, prior to departure to the USA. The photograph was taken at Southampton in 1939.

National Railway Museum, York

results, either experimentally or in every-day service until the early fifties at the Rugby testing station, the results of which are discussed later.

Possibly one of the more famous journeys made by a 'Duchess' was the visit to the 1939 World Fair in New York, with the addition of running over the tracks of eight USA railroads. The US railroad companies were very interested in the 'Coronation Scot' and approached the LMS with the suggestion that a complete train should be exhibited at the World Fair and also tour the eastern part of the USA. The LMS was in total agreement with the idea and a set of the latest vehicles was prepared for the visit.

Both the locomotive and the coaches were in red and gold rather than the original blue of the first streamlined members of the class. The reason for this livery was more to do with the locomotive supplied for the visit than any aesthetic reasons. *Duchess of Hamilton* was used for the trip, as she was a recent build and was felt to be in a more pristine condition, but of course she was completed in the original colour scheme of red and gold. Consequently, the names and numbers of Nos 6220 *Coronation* and 6229 *Duchess of Hamilton* were changed, so that the latter became No. 6220 *Coronation* for the duration of the USA trip. She was also compatible in terms of colour with the new streamlined coaching stock.

The train consisted of eight coaches of the new streamlined stock. All, apart from the sleeping car and club saloon, were articulated in pairs on three four-wheeled bogies. The sleeping car had six-wheel bogies and the club car four-wheel bogies. The rake consisted of a corridor 1st class brake, corridor 1st class, corridor 1st class lounge, 1st class diner, kitchen car, 3rd class diner, sleeping car and club saloon. The whole train was air-conditioned throughout, with adjustment to provide both warm and cool air. The total tare weight was 262 tons. The locomotive was fitted with a bell and electric headlight to meet US regulations. In addition, No. 6229 was fitted with a spark arrester, turbo generator and an automatic coupler. The automatic warning system was not fitted, even though this was becoming standard on US railroads. This, plus the UK standard vacuum braking system as opposed to air brakes as fitted to US locomotives, was probably the reason for the speed restrictions placed on the 'Coronation Scot' while in the US.

The train was the responsibility of R.A. Riddles, with Driver F.C. Bishop and Fireman J. Carswell on the footplate. Additionally, a Crewe works foreman, F.W. Soden, travelled as master 'mechanic'. It is interesting to compare the limited number of staff given to support the technical aspects of this visit with a similar type of visit today, when electrical engineers, computer experts, mechanical engineers, operating experts and train crews would all be involved.

Prior to departing the UK the train was exhibited at Euston and an official luncheon held to wish the team well, and to thank all those who built the locomotive and coaches. The train was hauled dead to Southampton where it was loaded aboard the Norwegian ship *Belpamela* on 20 January 1939, the *Bel* ships of the Christian-Smith line being the only shipping company with vessels big enough to handle a cargo of this size. A special track had been laid on the quayside at Southampton and this had been tested by a Southern Railway 'Lord Nelson' class. *Coronation*, the tender and one coach were stowed in the hold and the rest of the coaches were carried as deck cargo. Bad weather and a late departure from Southampton delayed arrival at Baltimore by six days. Riddles and the enginemen had previously travelled by transatlantic liner and were already there to receive and prepare the train for the start of the 3,120 mile tour. This commenced with a special VIP viewing on 17 March 1939.

One early problem occurred when the driver became seriously ill with pneumonia and was laid up for a month, and it was at this time that Riddles elected to carry out most of the firing for the early part of the visit. The visit was to include trips across the Baltimore and Ohio; Pennsylvania; Louisville and Nashville; Alton; New York Central and New York, New Haven and Hartford railroads. In this way cities as far apart as Baltimore, Washington, Philadelphia, Pittsburgh, Cincinnati, Louisville, Chicago, Detroit, Cleveland, Buffalo, Albany, Boston and Hartford were visited, a journey that took from 21 March until 14 April 1939.

During the first press run between Baltimore and Washington, various photographic stops were made, and at one time *Coronation* was dwarfed by the Baltimore and Ohio diesel locomotive *President Lincoln*. It was a hard day,

No. 6220 *Coronation* at Chicago Union station on 2 April 1939, during the visit to the USA. (Note the louvres in front of the cylinders showing that this is really No. 6229 *Duchess of Hamilton*.) The locomotive is fitted with both a bell and a large headlamp to meet USA regulations. The lady standing in the foreground does not seem to be too impressed.

National Railway Museum, York

starting at 06.00 and finishing at around 22.30, and when the train returned to Baltimore the quantity of coal used came as a nasty shock to Riddles and the enginemen. Some 11–12 tons had been used during the day, for a total mileage of approximately 150 miles. Riddles is quoted as saying at the presidential address to the Junior Institute of Engineers, 'and that [coal] provided at Baltimore by our standards was little more than slack'. This was not untypical of the type of fuel normally used for automatic stokers, something fairly common on USA railroads but unusual on UK or European railways. Consequently, while Riddles was dismayed with the quality, it would have been the norm for the Baltimore locomotives.

The host railroad, the Baltimore and Ohio, had taken a great deal of care to arrange a successful tour and probably never had a train received so much publicity and hospitality. The train left Baltimore on Tuesday 21 March 1939 at 10.00 precisely, set by the time signal initiated at the World Fair in New York. Everywhere the train stopped it was met by vast crowds, bands and the full American festive celebrations, and Riddles always made sure that the local mayor was on hand to open the exhibition. The train finally came to rest at the Fairground in New York at 23.00 on 14 April 1939.

The train performed very well mechanically, with few problems of any significance. The main difficulties centred round the firebrick arch which had to

A 'Coronation' club saloon of the type shipped to the USA, seen here in a publicity shot for
the exhibition at Euston in January 1939.

National Railway Museum, York

be renewed twice during the visit, the second time because of poor fitting of the
first replacement when the original arch started to fail at Harrisburg. Riddles
himself entered the firebox to assist in carrying out these repairs, and with the
help of the local boilermaker dismantled the arch during the early hours. He
returned to his hotel and after 3 hours' sleep attended the exhibition and then
rebuilt the arch that afternoon. During this period there was still 50 lb per sq. in
of steam in the boiler. But the train did depart on time at 21.00 that evening.

Again quoting Riddles from his presidential address to the Junior Engineering
Institute:

> . . . and suffice it to say that 3 hours of heaving lumps of firebrick, some
> weighing 25 lb and others up to 80 lb (the whole arch weighs 17 cwt) inside
> an engine firebox with 50 lb pressure of steam all round you, is an experience
> not readily to be forgotten! However, the job was finished by 5 p.m., and an
> hour or so later the fire was in again and all going well. Another bath, a
> rump steak and a bottle of Champagne, and bed. By 9 p.m. I was driving the
> train away to Springfield.

A 'Coronation Scot' vestibule first No. 7507. Originally built for general service by Wolverton Carriage Works in 1934, as lot 734, the carriage was subsequently converted for the 'Coronation Scot' trains, at Wolverton in 1937.

National Railway Museum, York

Other problems experienced needed less drastic actions, although a broken carriage spring bolt required the turning of a valve spindle of a similar tensile strength to replace the defective item. The elimination of the banging noise coming from below the sleeping car, once it was identified, took just 15 minutes to fix by adjustment of the spring. This caused amazement among the American fitters, who were used to fixed links.

During one evening run, after a busy day, *Coronation* was running at between 70 and 75 m.p.h. when a red flare was sighted at Plainview. A red flare is a US method of giving warning of an emergency sighted by the running crews. With a firm application of the brake and the rapid shutting of the regulator, the train came to a stand some 300 yd from a motor car which was straddling the track. The train was brought slowly up to the obstruction where a very shocked gentleman informed the crew that his car was stuck. Riddles and the footplate crew got the man back into his seat and with much heaving and pushing managed to release him from his predicament, not without much burning of tyre rubber. Riddles was quoted as saying later that the train proceeded to its next destination 'perhaps a little bit more soberly'.

Driver Bishop returned to driving on 9 April, as prior to that Riddles and Fireman Carswell had both driven and fired. But it took some time for Carswell to get used to the fact that white signals meant a clear road, despite the conductor driver calling out the aspects as the journey progressed.

The tour was a great success and more than two million people inspected the train on the tour and at the World Fair. During the time *Coronation* was in New York the Second World War broke out and it was decided that too much risk was entailed in bringing the train back to the UK, and in any case shipping space was now at a premium. Consequently, the locomotive went to Baltimore where it was stored and the train to Jeffersonville, Indiana, where it was used as living quarters for the US Army Quartermaster Corps. By 1942 it was considered that the risk was sufficiently diminished to ship the locomotive home again and on 16 February 1942 *Coronation* arrived back at Cardiff and travelled by the GWR to Crewe. She re-entered traffic on 18 March 1942, but the name-plates and numbers were not exchanged until 20 April 1943, when she entered Crewe works for repairs, at which time *Coronation* became the real *Duchess of Hamilton* again. This delay before the original identity was restored could explain the differences between various sources for the date of the locomotive's return to the UK, which has been stated as both 1942 and 1943. The chime whistle fitted to the locomotive for the US tour was installed at the Crewe locomotive works. The coaches did not return to the UK until after the war, in 1946.

In the years up to the Second World War a number of runs were monitored with 'Duchesses' on the 'Coronation Scot' service to Glasgow, as would be expected with a new locomotive on such a high-profile service. A typical run included No. 6220 *Coronation*, complete with dynamometer car, hauling the Down 'Coronation Scot' in November 1937, with a trailing load of 331 tons tare or 345 tons gross, including the dynamometer. The total coal consumption for the 401½ mile journey was 7 tons or 39.2 lb per hour and 3.03 lb per drawbar horsepower hour. The *average* drawbar horsepower over the complete journey was 825. These figures show what a sound and competent design the 'Duchesses' were.

The 'Coronation Scot' services from London and Glasgow were scheduled to start simultaneously from both cities at 13.30, with the intention to arrive at the other city by 20.00. The departure time was that normally occupied by the 'Midday Scot' service, or what had been known as the 'Corridor Express'. While it was advertised as a non-stop service, in fact there was a 2 minute stop for a crew change just outside Carlisle, at 18.13 to 18.15 on the Down train and 15.15 to 15.17 on the Up. The crews for this service were from the top link at Camden and Carlisle (Upperby) for the southern sections of the runs, and for the northern runs men from Glasgow (Polmadie) worked through with the locomotives.

The first public service commenced from both London and Glasgow on 5 July 1937 and drew a considerable number of spectators both to Euston and to Glasgow Central. It is probably unsurprising that both of the trains on this inaugural day arrived early and were to schedule during the journey. The Down train was met by Sir Josiah Stamp at Glasgow 4 minutes early, hauled by No. 6220 *Coronation* and driven by Driver D. Kerr, with Fireman H. Shelden on the northern run from Carlisle to Glasgow. The Up service arrived at Euston 2 minutes early and was hauled by No. 6221 *Queen Elizabeth*. The footplate

No. 46245 *City of London* passing Willesden in 1959 with the 'Caledonian' service. She is seen here in immaculate condition in BR red livery.

Rex Conway

crew for the Up run were Driver J. Curran and Fireman H. Scott from Carlisle to Euston and Driver Kerr and Fireman Shelden from Glasgow to Carlisle. The newspapers of the day suggested that the northern crew averaged 70 m.p.h. from Glasgow to Beattock and 82 m.p.h. from the summit of Beattock to Lockerbie, a not inconsiderable feat considering the gradients and amount of hill-climbing on this part of the LMS.

The first passenger to purchase a reserved ticket for the Up service was quoted in A.J. Mullay's book *Streamlined Steam* as being Mr Arthur Findley, a Glaswegian businessman living in Essex. He had left home at 21.45 the previous day to travel to Glasgow and after a morning of business meetings returned home, arriving at 21.00. While these are not brilliant timings compared with today's daily flights and hourly rail services to the North, it was a significant improvement over previous journeys, particularly considering the reliability of the 'Coronation Scot' with its consistent on-time arrivals.

The 'Coronation Scot' service was hauled exclusively by streamlined 'Duchesses' and operated five days a week, although the coaching stock was used for the Saturday and Sunday Llandudno expresses in the summer. This did tend to lessen the exclusive nature of the train even though it helped increase the economy of the vehicle use.

The punctuality of the service was almost 100 per cent with typically every arrival in September 1937 arriving on or ahead of time. As some indication of the service that the 'Duchesses' performed, a couple of Down runs are worthy of note. No. 6220 *Coronation*, having lost 85 seconds for an emergency stop at Rugby to clear a sander and then being 3½ minutes late at Carnforth, made up the arrears by a good climb to Shap Summit which was passed at 36 m.p.h. and arrived at Carlisle marginally early but 10 minutes ahead in terms of net timings. The following day, on the second run, speeds of 90 m.p.h. were achieved at least twice, and although Preston was passed just over 2 minutes late, the locomotive, No. 6221 *Queen Elizabeth*, had no difficulty with Shap and arrived at Carlisle exactly on time.

Records of journeys from Carlisle to Glasgow show that these locomotives had no in-service problems with Beattock and dealt with 'the long drag' with hardly a pause. Typically, No. 6220 crossed Beattock Summit after 12 miles of climbing, which included nearly 10 miles at 1 in 80, after running the 49.7 miles from Carlisle to Beattock in 46½ minutes, at an average 64.20 m.p.h., giving a very commendable performance.

One interesting run, again revealed in A.J. Mullay's book, was the special train for the King of Bulgaria, who was a great railway enthusiast. He was given a footplate run from Euston to Bletchley and back. The run took place on 5 November 1937, was hauled to Bletchley by No. 6220 and included the 'Coronation Scot' coaching set. The return run was carried out using 'Royal Scot' No. 6415 *The Duke of Wellington's Regiment (West Riding)*, presumably for the sake of variety. *Coronation* completed the run in 45 minutes, an average speed of 62.4 m.p.h. over the 46.7 mile journey, and achieved a maximum speed of 88 m.p.h. It is not recorded whether the king appreciated the finer points of the 'Duchesses', but in any case he was to die under mysterious circumstances during a visit to Hitler in 1943.

Two other unusual events related to the 'Coronation Scot' occurred prior to the Second World War. The first was on 8 November 1937, when the Up service was diverted via the Settle and Carlisle line because the normal route was blocked at Milnthorpe. No. 6221 *Queen Elizabeth* was replaced at Carlisle by Upperby 'Jubilee' class No. 5604 *Ceylon*, which hauled the 'Coronation Scot' through the Pennines via Hellifield and Blackburn, then subsequently regained its original route. The second was when No. 6220, aka No. 6229, was involved in one of the few failures of the 'Coronation Scot' service. On the Up service on 20 July 1939, the locomotive was stopped at Tring with a hot axlebox and was removed from the train. The substitute locomotive was Fowler 2–6–4T No. 2354, with Driver Grives at the regulator. The tank locomotive covered the remaining 31.7 miles to Euston in 34 minutes, an average speed of 55.8 m.p.h., a highly creditable performance. The high levels of workmanship at Crewe works and the tighter tolerances demanded by Stanier, including the good quality finishes of precision axleboxes and journals, meant that no scraping or fitting was needed, or allowed, and the occurrence of hot boxes on large passenger locomotives was significantly reduced. Consequently, this failure was an unusual event for the period.

City of Coventry at Carlisle, waiting to take the Edinburgh relief service to Birmingham on 28 December 1963.

John Wickham

The five streamlined locomotives built in 1938 and bearing the red and gold livery were intended for the non- 'Coronation Scot' services, in particular the schedules on the London–Merseyside services. Contemporary belief was that the change in livery was to retain the special effect and 'presence' of the streamliners, with the gold chevron and lines along the side of the locomotive, but to couple this with the flexibility of using the standard LMS maroon coaches. Around this time, consideration was given to chancing the livery of all the 'Coronation Scot' trains to red and gold, including the first five locomotives, but the advent of the Second World War stopped the change. This could have presented an interesting spectacle, with a blue and silver 'Duchess' hauling the special 'Coronation Scot' coaching stock in red and gold, prior to the locomotives being repainted.

The 'Duchesses' were a natural choice for the royal trains on the West Coast Main Line and were always superbly cleaned and groomed for this service, but it was a somewhat strange sight to see a streamlined blue and silver 'Duchess' at the head of the royal train coaches of clerestory design finished in LNWR plum and spilt milk livery.

As part of the improvements for the 'Coronation Scot' services, the track between London and Glasgow had to be improved so that fifty areas of speed restrictions were eliminated or the limits decreased. Typically, curves which had been designed for trains travelling at 60–70 m.p.h. now had to be modified to allow 90 m.p.h. In addition, platforms had to be altered and other loading gauge restrictions modified as much as possible. In some cases the LMS had to buy out landowners' mining rights so as to stop further removal of coal under the tracks because of the risks of subsidence. This was especially so at Polesworth. Interestingly, one area that had to wait until British Rail could modify the layout was Crewe, where a 20 m.p.h. limit was set for passing trains. The improvements to the West Coast Main Line are a legacy that has extended over the years to benefit the modern rail traveller. It could be argued that today's 100 m.p.h.-plus InterCity trains would have had a longer and more costly gestation period if the 'Duchesses' had not been running on the West Coast Main Line.

With the events leading up to the latter part of 1939, British railway companies started to put into effect their plans for war, with the slowing of services in general and increase of freight traffic. The golden age of streamlined express services was coming to an end.

CHAPTER SIX

THE WARTIME 'DUCHESSES'

On 3 September 1939 the then prime minister, Neville Chamberlain, broadcast to the nation just after 11.00, with the quietly read but chilling words, '. . . and that consequently this country is at war with Germany'. It was with this radio broadcast that the golden era of the railways ended for ever. The changes brought about by the war were to have an effect on the transport system of Great Britain which is still being felt today.

To understand the work and history of the 'Duchesses' during the war it is worth digressing slightly to appreciate the restrictions and changes which were to encompass the length and breadth of the railways, not just the LMS. Two days before the war started, on 1 September the Ministry of Transport made an order under the Emergency Powers (Defence) Act 1939 taking full control of the four British Railway companies. The Railway Executive Committee was formed to run the railways during the period of the order. The immediate effect was a general reduction in passenger services as from 11 September 1939, and it is probably not surprising that it was some time before the system truly settled down. The organization was faced with the possibility of mass civilian evacuation, air raids, the blackout and a large increase in freight and military traffic, so it was understandable that the situation became confused at times.

Plans for the evacuation had been detailed some months before the war started, but even with this preplanning the intention to move 4 million mothers and children from the threatened industrial and urban areas was a massive organizational undertaking. That it was completed without major difficulties is indicative of the skills and abilities of the railways and their staff.

The effect of the evacuation on passenger services can be judged from the poster which was displayed at all stations from 31 August 1939:

RAILWAY PASSENGER SERVICES DURING EVACUATION

The Mainline railways announce that during Excavation, alterations to the existing services will be necessary, and the public are requested to limit their train travel to essential journeys.

London Suburban Services – Before 8 a.m. and after 5.30 p.m. services will be as near as possible normal. Between 8 a.m. and 5.30 p.m. skeleton services will operate.

Provincial Suburban Services – During the hours of the evacuation, skeleton services only will operate.

Mainline Services – The Railways expect to maintain Mainline Services but no guarantee can be given as extensive alterations to **existing** timetables may have to be made without further notice.

In practice, during the early days both suburban and main-line travellers suffered little inconvenience, although later during the Blitz major disruptions were bound to be felt. Main-line express services had been decelerated quite dramatically by 11 September and most excursion and reduced-fare facilities were withdrawn. Speeds were not meant to exceed 60 m.p.h. and start/stop times were typically limited to 45 m.p.h. In addition, restaurant and buffet car services initially ceased as well, though from this distance it is difficult to see how their withdrawal would have helped the war effort. Gradually the meal services were returned in a limited manner and standard meals were introduced for 2s. 2½d.

The blackout regulations included all tender locomotives as well as the coaching stock. Tender locomotives were fitted with canvas screens which covered the space between the tender and firebox in an attempt to reduce the glare from the firebox at night. All coaches had the windows fitted with blinds and in the early stages blue lights were fitted, though these were subsequently changed to allow dim white reading lights. These were in effect a box over the central compartment light, fitted with strategically placed slots, which allowed some light to fall onto each seat.

There is photographic evidence to suggest that some of the 'Duchesses' were out-shopped from Crewe with the side windows blacked out, but it is difficult to understand the practical advantages of this, bearing in mind that crews would have to open these as part of normal driving operations. In any case the amount of additional light from these windows compared with that which could be seen via the gap between the tender and cab must have been limited.

Footplate crew and all railway operating staff were issued with 'tin hats' and gas masks, and all signal lamps were hooded. Further, the station lamps were modified so that the light shone down on the platforms only. Later, all stations had their nameboards painted out, reduced in size or made less easy to view. These were part of the precautions against both air raids and German invasion. Obviously this tended to make travel to unfamiliar areas difficult, to say the least, reliance being made on the calls of the porters at each stop. Additionally, all destination boards on coaches were removed, which no doubt led to many a wrong arrival caused by travelling in the wrong coach. Another effect of the onset of war was that the major railway companies moved their headquarters to areas considered to be less at risk. The LMS moved to Watford.

One surprising result of the reduction of train services early in the war was the increased number of cleaners available on the sheds, which coupled with more shed time meant that locomotives were kept in almost pristine condition. Operating staff

No. 46240 *City of Coventry* hauling the 10.00 Up 'Royal Scot' service from Euston, near South Dulton Viaduct on 8 August 1959.

M.H. Walshaw, Hugh Davis Collection

reported that Camden had a great selection of gleaming Pacifics, 'Royal Scots' and other locomotives. The succession of clean locomotives which were used to haul services all over the system was a real bonus to both traveller and enthusiast. However, this was to change as the war progressed, so much so that in March 1943 the *Railways Magazine* reported that after a five-day period of observations only four locomotives were seen that matched their prewar cleanliness. All the others were covered in a thick layer of grease and soot, and even the 'Duchesses' were not spared this fate. The dirty covering was known as 'austerity rust'.

The reasons for the eventual lack of cleanliness can best be understood by recognizing the extremely heavy traffic volumes that the railways had to deal with during the war years. Kenneth Oldham, in his book *Steam in Wartime Britain*, gives the following figures for typical railway traffic. During 1942 the LMS was involved in 1.713 million loaded wagon miles, an increase of some 34 per cent over the prewar years. This amount of traffic involved the use of 390,000 wagons per week to move the traffic originating on the LMS alone. The locomotives covered 121 million miles hauling freight, some 19 million more than in 1938. Further, an additional 55 million passenger journeys were made in 1942 than in 1941, an increase of 50 million journeys on the prewar figure. This was despite the government campaign to limit journeys to those essential by the 'Is your journey really necessary?' posters. Nearly five hundred special trains, both freight and passenger, ran each week in addition to the normal timetabled trains. Of the

No. 46223 *Princess Alice* hauling the 10.15 Glasgow to Euston service past the Chester main-line bridge near Norton on 29 August 1959.

M.H. Walshaw, Hugh Davis Collection

27,000 trains run each day by the LMS, 17,000 were freight, moving nearly 3 million tons of munitions and merchandise daily. It is worth noting that this traffic was consistent through the war, day in, day out. Consequently, it is not surprising that locomotive stock and track began to suffer, not just because of the huge increase in traffic but also because of the inevitable decrease in the numbers of skilled and qualified staff across the whole system.

The quality of services can best be summed up by a further quote from Kenneth Oldham's book, quoting part of a speech made by the chairman of the LMS, Sir Thomas Roydon Bt:

> The country as a whole is now reaping the benefit of a first-class railway system which in prewar days was built up by private enterprise in the face of strong competition and out-of-date legislation.

It was against this background that the 'Duchesses' operated throughout the war, producing sterling results.

A further aspect of the war was the impact the lack of basic materials had on the ability to maintain the locomotive stock successfully. As a result, scrapping limits for the various parts were revised early on during the war in order to give increased life between renewals. Typically, large axles were allowed to wear ³/₄ in below the original journal diameter, in contrast to the prewar figure of $1/2$ in. This principle was applied to tyres, piston rods, valve spindles, etc. Of course, the down side to this strategy was that the works had to carry a greater stock of larger sizes of brasses, bushes, glands, etc.

During the Second World War thirteen additional 'Duchesses' were built at Crewe, nine of which were streamlined. Of the streamlined examples five appeared in the original streamlined livery of maroon and gold, while the balance, including the nonstreamlined members, were finished in wartime black livery. Full details of the build dates and liveries can be found in the appendices. Interestingly, three of the wartime-built 'Duchesses' entered service from new with second-hand boilers. These were Nos 6245 *City of London*, 6247 *City of Liverpool* and 6248 *City of Leeds*. They were fitted with the boilers from Nos 6223 *Princess Alice*, 6232 *Duchess of Montrose* and stock built in the early forties respectively.

After the initial severe reduction in maximum speeds, the principal routes were allowed a relaxation to 75 m.p.h. At the same time the LMS was advising its drivers to use the capacity of the locomotives to the utmost so that lost time could be made up. This request was met with varying degrees of interpretation by footplate crews. Some made little effort to improve on the scheduled point-to-point timings, while others ran up to the old prewar timings when able to make up time.

The daytime Anglo-Scottish express services were allowed 182 minutes for the 141 miles from Crewe to Carlisle. This was calculated as 66 minutes to Preston (51 miles), 33 minutes to Carnforth (27.3 miles) and 49 minutes for the 31.4 miles to Shap Summit. One particular trip, hauled by the nonstreamlined No. 6230 *Duchess of Buccleuch*, with a load of 500 tons, was so delayed as to take 73 minutes to pass Preston, but thereafter, even though the road was clear and the locomotive was in good condition, the driver made no attempt to gain time to Carlisle, instead doing no more than keeping to the sectional timings. By comparison, streamlined No. 6237 *City of Bristol* left Crewe 15 minutes late with a 475 ton train in early 1941, and but for a signal check outside Citadel station, Carlisle would have been reached early. Allowing for signal checks the net time for the run from Crewe to Carlisle was 157 minutes, some 25 minutes inside the schedule.

The route between Preston and Carlisle, when free of signal and traffic checks, saw many instances of exemplary running with heavy and crowded wartime trains. In particular, two further examples of 'Duchesses' on the Euston–Glasgow run are shown below. Both show that the performance of these locomotives was well up to prewar standards. The locomotives, streamlined No. 6221 *Queen Elizabeth* and nonstreamlined No. 6234 *Duchess of Abercorn*, were working through trains from Euston to Glasgow. The times from Carnforth to Shap Summit were 37 minutes 39 seconds and 40 minutes 7 seconds respectively. These gave average speeds of 50 and 47 m.p.h. respectively. The crews on these runs gave good examples of the wartime slogan 'going to it'.

LMS PRESTON TO CARLISLE, 1942

Locomotive No.				No. 6221		No. 6234	
Load tare/gross				480/525		499/560	
Distance			Scheduled	Actual		Actual	
miles			mins	mins	secs	mins	secs
00.0	Preston		0	0	00	0	00
21.0	Lancaster		26	24	27	26	32
27.3	Carnforth		33	30	15	32	03
40.1	Oxenholme		50	43	23	46	25
47.2	Grayrigg			53	18	57	04
53.2	Tebay		69	59	41	62	33
58.7	Shap Summit		81	67	54	72	10
72.2	Penrith		96	80	51	85	23
90.1	Carlisle		116	102	42	102	23
Net Running Times				96		98.5	

SPEEDS

	No. 6221	No. 6234
	m.p.h.	m.p.h.
Maximum before Carnforth	74	71.5
Minimum Grayrigg Summit	37	35.5
Minimum Shap Summit	30	22.5
Maximum down to Carlisle	79	80.5

One of the services on the Anglo-Scottish route which was of some interest was the so-called 'ghost train', running normally each night from both Euston and Glasgow St Enoch. The train became something of a celebrity when it was observed one night leaving Euston, although it was not shown on the timetable. When it was seen on further nights by the same observer he wrote to his MP and eventually a question was raised in the House of Commons. It turned out to be a train which was confined to service personnel and people on official government business. The southbound train left St Enoch at 21.27, called at Kilmarnock, and as far as the passengers were concerned made a non-stop journey to Watford Junction. However, there was actually a stop for a crew change at Carlisle with the non-stop section on to Watford Junction, a distance of 281½ miles, scheduled for 364 minutes, an overall speed of 46.4 m.p.h. The service was normally 'Duchess'-hauled.

O.S. Nock was granted permission by Ivatt to make a footplate run on the train from Glasgow to Carlisle, and he described it in his book, *A History of the LMS 1939–48*. The locomotive concerned was No. 6224 *Princess Alexandra*, the last of the original 1937 streamlined members of the class. The load was 463 tons tare and not more than 490 tons gross as the rake consisted of a number of sleeping cars. The route followed the former Glasgow and South Western Railway and included the very severe Neilstone bank. This begins just under 6½ miles from

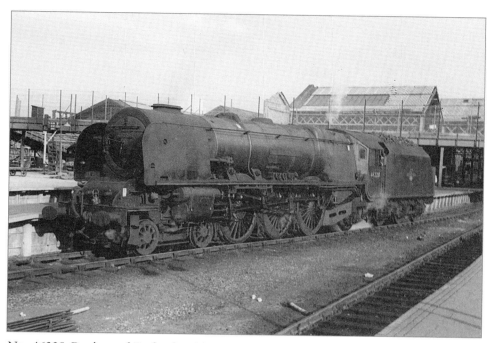

No. 46228 *Duchess of Rutland* waiting at Euston to work the 18.40 service to Inverness on 26 July 1963.

John Wickham

Glasgow and includes 3¼ miles of 1 in 67–70. Normally this would have necessitated a banker on heavy trains, but with the 'Duchesses' no such assistance was required. In fact, when adverse signals almost brought the train to a stand at Neilstone station, right on the 1 in 70 gradient, No. 6224 started away cleanly and without slipping when the signal was cleared, so much so that only 3 minutes were lost on leaving Kilmarnock. This deficit was made up by the time the train was approaching Dumfries, and it would have arrived 1 minute early but for the delay caused by the night service to St Pancras, which having left Glasgow 12 minutes ahead of the 'ghost train', was still in Dumfries station. The train arrived at Carlisle after the final section of the run was completed under easy steam, with the speed not exceeding 70 m.p.h.

The point-to-point timings were initially stiff on the first 21.1 miles to New Cumnock, the section that included all the heavy gradients. The overall timing for the 58 miles from Glasgow St Enoch to Dumfries was 72 minutes, with a timing of 30 minutes to New Cumnock. The next section timings were more favourable, with 42 minutes allowed for the 36.9 miles to Dumfries. The final 34.1 miles to a stop at Carlisle No. 12 box, where the crews were changed, was 48 minutes. *Princess Alexandra* completed this section in 46.4 minutes.

A further incident involving the 'ghost train' occurred during the early hours of Monday 15 May 1944, when No. 6225 *Duchess of Gloucester*, one of the original maroon and gold streamliners, was approaching Mossband signal-box at high speed with the 20.20 service from Euston to Glasgow. All of a sudden the locomotive left the rails. Three service personnel were killed in the accident. One, an American serviceman, was found to have been standing in the front coach and had suffered a heart attack. The fireman of the train, Jack Graham, was awarded the Josiah Stamp Medal for his diligence in protecting his train, under rule 55, despite his injuries. The driver, Willie Mitchenson, was having his first turn at the regulator of a 'Duchess' and while surviving the accident, he eventually died from its longer-term effects. One of the factors that most certainly enabled both members of the footplate crew to survive the accident was that the locomotive had been on a through working from London and was not just off Kingmoor shed. If the latter had been the case then no doubt both crew would have been crushed by the tender emptying its full load of coal over the footplate. The enquiry into the accident put the cause down to faulty track.

As the war progressed and victory became more likely, the demands on the railways increased and as part of this effort the works contributed by producing a host of military products, including tanks, guns and aircraft. In addition, the track layouts themselves were increased to include new military camps, armament dumps and munition works, with the addition of new junctions and various sidings. The works were encouraged to salvage all waste material, so much so that in the first three years of the war Crewe was able to reclaim 8,820 tons of materials, of which 8,375 tons were used within the works. All these changes had a severe effect on both the serviceability and timings of train services, despite the special efforts of railwaymen.

From 1943 plain black livery became the standard for British locomotives as a wartime expedient to cut down on maintenance and costs, and the 'Duchesses' followed suit. The first locomotives to appear in this livery were the four streamliners Nos 6245–8 *Cities of London, Manchester, Liverpool* and *Leeds*. These were built in 1943 and were constructed in wartime black from new. The nonstreamlined *Cities of Sheffield, Lichfield, Nottingham* and *Leicester*, built in 1944, were also delivered with wartime black livery from new. The balance of the class had the new livery applied at the time of wartime overhauls. The only members of the class which were not painted black were Nos 6230/33/34, *Duchesses of Buccleuch, Sutherland* and *Abercorn*, which were built in 1938 with a Midland red livery and were nonstreamlined. No reasons can be found as to why these members of the class were not painted in wartime black, but it may have been due to the locomotives not returning for major overhauls at convenient times or perhaps temporary wartime shortages.

While the LMS didn't lose any of its Pacifics due to bomb damage, unlike the LNER, one incident is worth recording. The 10.00 train from Euston, hauled by No. 6232, the nonstreamlined *Duchess of Montrose*, was badly damaged by

No. 46245 *City of London* seen at her home shed, Willesden, on 26 January 1964.
John Wickham

fallen girders after the Rose Lane bridge at Berkhamsted was struck by Nazi bombs on 16 November 1940. Incredibly, nobody was hurt in the incident.

Two further incidents during the war years are worthy of note, and both tragically involved loss of life. The first concerned No. 6224 *Princess Alexandra* on the morning of 10 September 1940, when the firebox crown was inadvertently left uncovered, with dire results. Driver Smith was injured and his fireman died in the resulting steam explosion. The enquiry found that both the footplate crew were inexperienced with the class and had only joined the locomotive 3 minutes before departure from Glasgow. The train was the 10.00 from Glasgow to Euston and the accident occurred on the climb up to Craigenhall, between Cleghorn and Carstairs. Coincidentally, a further accident involving this locomotive occurred in similar circumstances at almost the same spot some eight years later. A part of the firebox collapsed and steam at 250 lb per sq. in was released into the cab, killing Driver J. Wheaton and seriously injuring Fireman J. Wilson.

The second serious wartime incident, at Ecclefechan, led to a fairly striking modification to the 'Duchesses' with the addition of smoke deflector plates. (It is the opinion of the author that the smoke deflectors enhanced the appearance of the locomotives, making more aesthetically pleasing and creating a stronger sense of power and purpose.) The accident happened when No. 6231 *Duchess of Atholl* collided with a goods train which was setting back into the sidings. Ecclefechan is the first station south of Lockerbie. The 'Duchess' was hauling the 13.00 train from Glasgow to Euston on 21 July 1945 and was travelling at between 60 and 65 m.p.h. at the time of impact. The locomotive was seriously damaged and ended up laying on its right side some 138 yd ahead of the point of impact. Both the footplate crew were killed in the accident but thankfully no passengers were killed, and even though thirty-one were injured all left hospital within ten days. It was considered that the distance the train travelled after the impact probably saved many lives. The goods train locomotive was pushed forward some 100 yd and the energy absorbed in this action was significant.

The cause of the accident was the express overrunning all the signals on the approach to Ecclefechan. The Distant was set at caution and the outer and inner Home signals were set at stop. Why this occurred will never be known for sure because of the death of both crew, but the inspecting officer from the Ministry of Transport did confirm that the signals were operating correctly and that the Distant signal was sufficiently to the rear of the Home signals to allow braking from a speed of 60–65 m.p.h. Evidence was given that a thick pall of smoke was seen clinging to the locomotive, thereby obscuring the view of the driver.

A short time after this accident, O.S. Nock was riding on the footplate of No. 6251 *City of Nottingham* on a damp night, with the exhaust beating down on the boiler so much as to seriously obscure the view ahead. Observation was so bad that the driver was shutting off the steam to enable him to see the signals. It was under similar conditions that the accident at Ecclefechan occurred. Nock was so concerned that he felt moved to write directly to Ivatt expressing his fears and concerns.

'Duchesses' were fitted with smoke deflectors from 1945 to 1946, and all previous streamlined versions were fitted at conversion to nonstreamlined versions. Likewise the last two 'Duchesses' to be built, No. 6256 *Sir William A. Stanier FRS* and No. 46257 *City of Salford*, were fitted from new, as were Nos 6253–5 *Cities of St Albans, Stoke-on-Trent* and *Hereford*. Although No. 6232 *Duchess of Montrose* and No. 6252 *City of Leicester* were fitted with smoke deflectors as an experiment in February and March 1945 following works orders issued in September 1944, contemporary information shows that while this information was available it was the results of the Ecclefechan accident that polarized the situation.

As the war progressed, skilled crews and shed staff lost members to the war effort and the armed forces, which in turn meant that a greater number of less-experienced crews were moved up the ladder to the higher links of the various sheds. One of these was George Bushell of Willesden shed, who recalls in his book *Willesden Footplate Memories* that while the Camden turntable was being overhauled it meant that Willesden men were relieving main-line crews at Euston. It was because of this that, 'I managed to lay my hands on the regulator of No. 6247 *City of Liverpool*. After some of the rough engines that we had been used to, this big, well-kept Pacific really seemed like the Rolls Royce of the engine

No. 46247 *City of Liverpool* hauling an Up express at speed. In this view the advantages gained from fitting the smoke deflectors can be clearly seen; how well the smoke is lifted away from the footplate.

National Railway Museum, York

world. . . . I remember it was a great feeling to sense the power from the four cylinders.'

The wartime long-distance passenger services were invariably heavily loaded, in terms of both carriages hauled and the number of passengers carried. This was particularly the case on the Euston to Glasgow routes, where servicemen of all nationalities, particularly American, were travelling back and forth from the capital to the various training and disembarkation points in Scotland. This became doubly the case with the build-up to D-Day. The gradients on the West Coast Main Line were severe and these heavily loaded trains were liable to extreme delays because of the loads hauled. With lesser locomotives it was normal for bankers to be attached to give assistance, particularly at Shap and Beattock, though this was not considered the done thing for 'Duchesses'. Many a member of the class conquered the heights of Shap without assistance, but sometimes things did go wrong.

Halfway up the 1 in 75 Shap gradient was the signal-box of Scout Green. This controlled the level-crossing at this point and two signals in each direction. The box also acted as an intermediate block post. During 1942, the 10.00 train from Euston, hauled by a streamlined 'Duchess' (the name and number shall remain anonymous to save the embarrassment of the locomotive) was climbing Shap with a seventeen-coach train, grossing around 600 tons. As the train approached Scout

Green the driver saw that the Home signal was at danger, the train speed was rapidly reduced and it approached the signal at walking pace. At the same time the signalman was anxiously watching his block instruments for the train out of section indication but this came too late and the train had to come to a full stop before the signal was pulled off.

The driver now had to attempt to get the train underway once more, but even though conditions were good, the locomotive could not lift the train, despite the sanders being tried. The signalman knew his job and within 15 minutes the banker from Tebay had arrived and with the banker attached at the rear, the train moved slowly forward, making for the summit.

It is a curious fact that some locomotives become more well known than others. This was for various reasons, some more obvious than others, and clearly No. 6220 *Coronation* was famous as the first of the class and for holding the steam record, albeit for a short time only. Others, like No. 6224 *Princess Alexandra*, with the two fatal accidents involving firebox failures, became notorious, while No. 6234 *Duchess of Abercorn* displayed immense power over Beattock Summit in the loading trials just before the war. It was *Duchess of Abercorn* which was also involved in an unusual incident at Watford Junction during 1945.

The train, a fourteen-coach fast express, was stopped at signals just outside the station on the Down fast road. As the signals changed, the locomotive regulator was opened and without reason jumped to full open and locked in that setting. The driver was unable to close the regulator or put the locomotive in midgear and consequently he had to move into the platform with the brakes full on and the wheels slipping. The coupled wheels were slipping so fast that before the footplate crew could deal with the problem and stop the wheels turning, the track had been severely damaged by friction. The track was so ground down that the main line had to be closed to all traffic until the rails had been replaced. The train was transferred to the slow line and continued its journey hauled by a 2–6–4 tank locomotive, No. 2444. *Duchess of Abercorn* was removed to a siding by another 2–6–4 tank, No. 2489.

Despite all the difficulties arising from the wartime restrictions of time and loadings the 'Duchesses' gave a good account of themselves in regular traffic, and one particular instance concerns No. 6244 *King George VI*, still at that time in streamlined form. The information was recorded by C.M. Furst and is recounted by O.S. Nock's biography of Sir William Stanier. The train was the 10.05 from Euston, loaded to 475 tons gross, which had been brought to a halt at the signals at Oxenholme South box. The footplate crew made a tremendous effort on restarting, and by noting the passing times at each milepost, Mr Furst was able to record a speed at Hay Fell of 59 m.p.h., on a gradient of 1 in 131, and Grayrigg summit was cleared at 57 m.p.h. – magnificent.

Many anecdotal stories have been told about the wartime LMS in general and the 'Duchesses' in particular. One concerns a heavily loaded express approaching London during an air raid, with passengers taking shelter at carriage floor level.

The locomotive crew decided to take shelter in the approaching tunnel and stay there until the worst had passed. Unfortunately, the train was of a sufficient length that while the crew and the front half of the train were protected by the tunnel, the rear portion of the train was left outside to experience the dangers of the Blitz. Thankfully, no serious injuries or damage were incurred and the express was eventually able to proceed to the London terminus. The locomotive is not known, other than it being a streamlined 'Duchess'.

As the war drew to a close so too did the period of constant threat from enemy action against railway installations. The era of long hours was coming to an end, and the beginnings of the human changes which were to have such a dramatic effect on the postwar railways were in sight. The status of railwaymen of all levels was changing and with it the morale of the individual, and while it is not the intention to discuss here the reasons for these changes, the results meant that never again would the railways produce the glamorous services hauled by the streamlined locomotives of the thirties. This special era of service provision is almost gone forever.

Despite all the problems of wartime railway operations, such as extreme loadings, limited maintenance, high mileage and poor quality fuel, the 'Duchesses' were still able to give a good account of themselves.

It was against this successful background that the postwar design improvements to the 'Duchess' class were to be made, which were to have a significant impact on future BR designs.

CHAPTER SEVEN

THE FINAL DESIGNS

In 1942 Stanier was seconded to the Ministry of Supply as scientific adviser, in 1943 he was knighted and made a fellow of the Royal Society, and subsequently formally resigned from the LMS in 1944. His influences, skills and qualities of leadership were to live on with his successors. The fact that he was able to leave the CME department at the LMS in such a well-organized and united condition has to rank as one of the major achievements of his time with the company. His successors carried forward his ideas during both the short time before nationalization and during the BR era, and his influences could be seen in the designs of the future BR Standard classes.

H.G. Ivatt became the last CME of the LMS and was appointed on the sad and unexpected early death of C.E. Fairburn, who had been appointed CME after Stanier's retirement. It is indicative of Stanier's organizational skills and management ability that the sudden death of his successor did not throw the mechanical engineering department into a crisis. The number of talented engineers on Stanier's staff ensured that the LMS management was able to nominate an experienced successor from the ranks of the CME's department. Ivatt was the son of the former Great Northern Railway CME.

The modifications to the last two 'Duchesses' were largely the responsibility of Ivatt. The intention was to apply the lessons learnt during the Second World War in achieving better servicing and to make detailed design changes so as to increase the annual mileage and the mileages between visits to the workshop. During the time the last two 'Duchesses' were being built, the LMS was also building the first two diesel-electric locomotives to operate on UK main-line services. These were Nos 10000 and 10001, and comparative trials were planned between the two latest Pacifics and the diesels on the West Coast Main Line. The two diesels worked some west coast trains but never made a real impact, as the situation changed with nationalization, and but for this it is possible that the LMS would have introduced diesel traction as early as the 1950s.

The aim was to achieve a locomotive capable of working 100,000 miles a year. Nos 6256 *Sir William A. Stanier FRS* and 46257 *City of Salford*, apart from some differences at the rear, were little changed in appearance from previous 'Duchesses'. Probably the most significant change was the use of grease-lubricated roller bearings on all the axleboxes, both on the locomotive and the tender. The

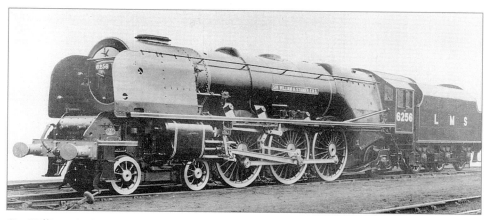

Sir William A. Stainier FRS, No. 46256, in LMS livery, fitted with the original design of pony truck. Compare this photograph with the one on p. 123.

National Railway Museum, York

crank axle on the leading coupled wheels was fitted with Skefco self-aligning boxes which allowed the cranks to 'breathe'. The other boxes were fitted with Timken tapered roller bearings. Those on the bogie, intermediate and trailing coupled wheels were of the split-cannon type and the remaining axles had individual bearing axleboxes.

An innovation for the LMS at this time, included on the new Pacifics, was the use of manganese steel liners on the axleboxes and horn guide faces. This had already proved of value during trials on other LMS locomotives, and had increased the mileage between shops, so much so that the life of other components now had to be increased to match the conditions of the axleboxes and tyres. The practice originated in the USA and was made known to Derby by the Timken company. A further change to the axle area was the use of frame clips, across the horn gaps, instead of the LMS standard keeps, which were extremely heavy, both to handle and fit. The frame clips were known as Horwich clips in the shops and were light bars, light enough to make the fitter's job that much easier. The motion was fitted with oil-lubricated steel bushes and case-hardened motion pins, and in addition ball bearings were fitted to the return cranks.

A further change to the normal LMS practice was the inclusion of rocking grates and self-emptying ashpans on the final 'Duchesses'. The rocking grate was almost a direct copy of the type fitted to the USA Army Transportation Corps 2–8–0 class, which operated in the UK during 1942–4. The grate consisted of two main sections which were laid side by side, divided into front, middle and rear parts. Each section could be rocked back and forth by the action of the footplate control gear. In addition, by lifting a restraining bracket the grate could be rotated through 90 degrees, thereby dropping the fire into the ashpan. The ashpan was

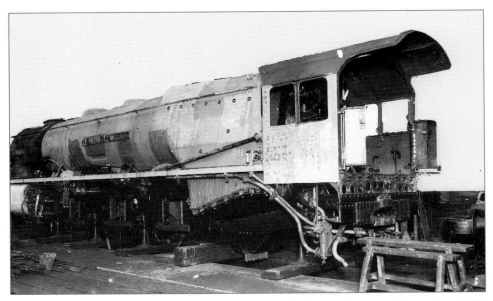

No. 46256 *Sir William A. Stanier FRS*, awaiting wheeling at Crewe in December 1947.
Note that the name-plate, cylinders, oil and sandboxes are fitted, and that cab boiler
fittings are also attached.

National Railway Museum, York

equipped with hopper doors which allowed the fire to be discharged to the
ashpits. The ashpan also had normal damper doors but these were controlled by a
hand wheel, which gave a more positive control, rather than the previous difficult
to operate notched levers.

Due to the significant design changes of the ashpan and grate, the opportunity
was taken to modify the trailing truck design and improve the trailing end
performance. The new trailing truck consisted of a one-piece cast-steel frame
which was known as a delta truck, and side control was provided by helical
springs. A further change was the modification to the rear frames. While these
were still attached to the mainframes behind the trailing coupled axleboxes, as on
previous members of the class, Nos 6256 and 46257 were fitted with a 2 in
semibar frame which was riveted on and supported the rear buffer beam. A pair
of support brackets transferred the weight to the new rear truck. The change to
the rear frames was an attempt to overcome the problems of cracks experienced
on the earlier design of the frame.

The redesign of the rear truck, frames and ashpan, meant that the cab side
sheets were reduced in depth, as well as lacking the curved fronts of the early
members of the class. The cab sides bore some similarity to the Ministry of Supply
2–8–0 locomotives and because of this the new Pacifics were known as 'Austerity
4–6–2s', a name which it is reputed was unknown outside the railway community.

Speedometer dial as fitted on the cab of *Sir William A. Stanier FRS*. Note also the forward and reverse gear control with the percentages marked on the vertical drum. The interior is shown here as fitted in February 1950.
National Railway Museum, York

A further change on the last two Pacifics was the new design of the reversing screw and cutoff indicator. The screw was fitted away from the traditional position, to a site located inside the frames next to the weighbar shaft. The screw was coupled by a tube and universal joints to the hand wheel in the cab, which was placed sideways to make it easier to operate. The tube could be seen above the running board on the left-hand side of the locomotive. The gear was indicated on a drum, with percentage markings, attached to the hand wheel. This arrangement was later adopted by BR on its Standard classes.

The smokebox on these Pacifics was fitted with wire mesh grids, removable for tube cleaning and giving a self-cleaning action for the smokebox. A new design of boiler top feed was installed, consisting of deflector plates in the form of a saddle over the tubes, rather than trays as in the original design. The intention was to deposit sludge at the bottom of the boiler, well clear of the tubes. The saddle also gave de-aeration action. How effective the new design was over the original is difficult to ascertain. No record can be found of whether, when the boilers were changed on Nos 6256 and 46257 at major overhaul, the changed boilers included the new design or whether boilers on other locomotives were retrospectively fitted with the changes. In its relatively short life, No. 6256 had four boiler changes and No. 46257 had three. However, it has been suggested that No. 6256 had an additional boiler change in 1962 which is not shown on the record cards.

The superheaters initially fitted were of the '5P4' type, which gave the largest superheating surface on any British locomotive, at 979 sq. ft. The '5P4' consisted of a single outward tube which split into four inside the flue tube and then

The original pony truck as fitted to No. 46256; compare this with the pony truck fitted to the original 'Duchesses' and also note the changes to this design when it was subsequently fitted to both *Sir William A. Stanier FRS* and the *City of Salford*, No. 46257. The pony truck is shown here at Crewe in December 1947.

National Railway Museum, York

returned as a single large-diameter central tube to the header. The four tubes were 1 in diameter and had external fins, and the return tube was $1\frac{1}{2}$ in. This type of superheater did not last long and it was replaced with the standard triple element type. This would suggest that no significant advantage was gained and the maintenance and stockholding of a different type, in limited numbers, could have led to cost disadvantages.

A new feature for the boiler was the use of a blow-off cock on the throatplate operated by a lever with a handle on both sides of the locomotive. The purpose was to discharge some of the sludge and scale from around the firebox. The cock was designed to be open for one minute on shed.

Initially, both Nos 6256 and 46257 were fitted with electric headlights as well as white discs for day use, but the equipment suffered a number of failures and was removed from the locomotives early in their career. The new Pacifics still experienced problems with the performance of the trailing truck and on No. 6256 the truck was ultimately changed to a fabricated version. Examination of the two locomotives shows significant differences in construction. The most obvious is the circular lightening hole, as opposed to the triangular hole as first fitted to the truck. This, plus the modified construction, makes the truck frame look very 'makeshift'. These changes only affected the truck. The axleboxes and rear frames

Smiths speedometer drive as fitted to No. 46256 *Sir William A. Stanier FRS*. The drive was taken from the rear driving wheel. Compare this drive with the original mechanical drive on the streamlined 'Duchesses'.

National Railway Museum, York

were not changed. Nothing was ever admitted by the officials about these changes but the locomotive spent 153 days in Crewe works between 16 February and 16 October 1948. Ultimately, No. 46257 was modified in the same manner.

Prior to the reassessment of the 'Duchesses' carried out by Ivatt, the last three 'standard-designed' members of the class were completed in 1946. These were Nos 6253–5 *Cities of St Albans*, *Stoke-on-Trent* and *Hereford*. All were built with self-cleaning smokeboxes, self-cleaning ashpans and rocking grates, similar to the changes on Nos 6256 and 46257. The use of self-cleaning smokeboxes had met with doubts as to the effectiveness of such devices, it being generally believed in Great Britain that a sharper blast would be needed to overcome any resistance to the gas flow. In fact the experience gained from Nos 6253–5 indicated that there was no appreciable difference and the locomotives were now able to run from one boiler washout day to the next without the firebox being opened – a very significant advantage.

As has already been discussed, smoke deflector plates were fitted to all the 'Duchesses' that were not fitted from new, starting with the nonstreamlined members of the class, Nos 6230/1/3/4 and 6249–51, Nos 6232 and 6252 having been fitted experimentally in early 1945. The deflectors were fitted between March and November 1946. As the streamlined members of the class had the aerodynamic casing removed, deflector plates were fitted. Initially, they did not have hand- or footholds, but because of the changes to the curved portion of the front end platforms, these were introduced across all of the class except Nos 6230–4 and 6249–52, which had retained the original curved section of the front platforms. The hand- and footholds were fitted to these when an order was issued in May 1955. It is interesting to note that while the removal of the curved section of the front platforms was for maintenance reasons, the original nonstreamlined members of the class which had retained the curved fronts had been fitted from new with hinged sections to allow easy access to the valve gear, the stated reason for the removal of the curves!

Clearly the change which had the most obvious impact was the removal of the streamlined casings. It was considered that the limited advantages of streamlining at higher speeds did not offset the increased problems caused during maintenance and servicing, or for that matter the small weight disadvantages. The removal of the casing helped to enhance and emphasize the handsome outlines of these locomotives.

The majority of the streamlined 'Duchesses' had their casings removed between April 1946 and December 1947, although No. 46243 *City of Lancaster* didn't have its casing removed until May 1949. This was the only streamlined 'Duchess' to operate in British Railways service. All the locomotives retained the sloping smokeboxes which were originally fitted to match the front shape of the streamlining. These were changed to standard smokeboxes starting with No. 46235 *City of Birmingham* in July 1952, and completed in May 1960 with No. 46246 *City of Manchester*. The changes were carried out as renewals for boilers became necessary. With the removal of the casing, the curved section of the footplate forward of the cylinders was left off the locomotives. It was felt that from a maintenance point of view cost savings could be made by giving better access to the valves, although aesthetically it tended to spoil the overall lines of the locomotives. Once 'defrocked' it was straightforward to recognize the former streamlined as opposed to the original nonstreamlined members of the class, as the latter still had the curved section fitted. One exception to this rule was No. 46242 *City of Glasgow*, when it returned to service following the extensive damage occasioned by the Harrow and Weldstone disaster. *City of Glasgow* was fitted with the traditional curved front end, thus making it unique among the former streamlined locomotives. The last three 'standard' 'Duchesses' built in 1946, Nos 6253–5, were all built from new with the curved section removed.

Not only was the streamlined casing removed from the locomotives, but changes were made to the tenders as well. In June 1943 instructions were given to remove the streamlined shroudings on the top of the tenders to increase the coal capacity. This work was completed by October 1943, in readiness for the

No. 6235 *City of Birmingham*, shown with sloping smokebox and with the short-lived, non-standard, Ivatt-designed chimney. The locomotive is seen here shortly after being 'defrocked'.

National Railway Museum, York

resumption of non-stop services from London to Glasgow. Tenders were recalled specially to complete this task. Prior to the locomotives being 'defrocked', orders had gone out to remove the extended sides on the streamlined tenders so as to ease tank filling. The removal of the covering along the lower side of the tender took place at the same time as the removal of the tender shrouds. It is unlikely that any work on the tenders, other than the shroud removal, was completed before the locomotives were 'defrocked'.

City of Birmingham was the first locomotive to have the casing removed and originally it was intended that the locomotive should return to service with the chimney fitted when it was first streamlined, which did not have the standard Stanier-style lip round the top. This was replaced before entering service and a standard-lipped double chimney, similar to that on the nonstreamlined members of the class, was fitted. All 'Duchesses' which had the casing removed were so fitted.

Ultimately, all 'Duchesses' were fitted with 'stink bombs' for detecting hot boxes, and also Automatic Warning System (AWS), although the latter was more as a result of the outcry over the Harrow accident. The LMS had carried out detailed trials of AWS on the London–Tilbury line, but the lack of progress was due to a general malaise among the railway companies, except the GWR, rather than any technical inability.

At the end of the Second World War, and during the early British Railways period, all the 'Duchesses' ran in one of the black liveries, either wartime black, LMS black or BR black, with one exception. In March 1946 No. 6234 *Duchess of Abercorn* was running in experimental grey livery, and then in May 1948 was initially repainted in experimental blue before joining the majority of the class, which by then had been painted in BR blue. It wasn't until the early fifties that the whole class was painted in the same colour, BR green. Details of the liveries can be found in the appendices.

Even though the majority of the locomotives named after cities had been built just before or during the war, in some cases naming ceremonies didn't take place until the latter part or the end of the war. The policy of the LMS was to have the ceremony at the city concerned, and consequently some locomotives travelled far from their normal routes. The ceremony for No. 6246 *City of Manchester* was held at Manchester Victoria station rather than the Exchange station (now Manchester Piccadilly). No. 6254 *City of Stoke-on-Trent* was only able to arrive at the city via Norton Bridge, as all other routes were prohibited. After the naming ceremony for No. 6251 *City of Nottingham*, the locomotive became derailed as it was leaving the Lincoln end of the station, causing extensive delays to traffic in the area. *Cities of Birmingham, Coventry* and *Stoke-on-Trent* were fitted with the city coat of arms on plaques above the locomotive name-plate. This practice was similar to the crown fitted over the nameplates of No. 6220 *Coronation*. The name-plates for No. 6249 *City of Sheffield* were manufactured by one of the Sheffield steel companies, made of stainless steel and fitted some two months after the naming ceremony.

While the last two 'Duchesses' were being built, decisions had to be made about their names. R.C. Bond has been quoted as saying that the decision for naming No. 6256 was taken during a journey from Derby to Crewe in the company of Riddles, then vice-president for engineering, and Ivatt, by then CME. The discussion centred on the names for the last two 'Duchesses' and concern was expressed at the risk of running out of city names. The suggestion was made of naming one *Sir William A. Stanier*. This was received with great acclaim and became the fifth of the famous Crewe 'black' locomotives to be named after a former CME. Formerly, John Ramsbottom had a Newton 2–4–0 named after him, Bowen-Cooke named the 'George the Fifth' class 4–4–0s after both Webb and George Whale, and one of the Claughton class was named after Bowen-Cooke himself. Incidentally, No. 6256 was the fiftieth Pacific to be built by the LMS, including the 'Princess Coronations' and the 'Turbomotive'.

The naming ceremony for No. 6256 took place at Euston at the same time as an exhibition of the new diesels was taking place, on 18 December 1947. The chairman of the LMS, Sir Robert Burrows, in the company of Sir William Stanier, officially named the locomotive prior to the opening of the exhibition. In carrying out the ceremony, Sir Robert commented that while he had named a number of locomotives after cities, regiments or colonies, this was the first time he had

City of Stoke on Trent, No. 46254, seen in immaculate condition at the Golden Jubilee Exhibition at Stoke on Trent. The ATC battery box and vacuum reservoir can be clearly seen on the running plate. Note also the city coat of arms above the name-plate.

National Railway Museum, York

named one after an individual. He went on to say, 'The LMS never had a better engine nor a better name connected with it.'

The performance of No. 6256 was recorded by O.S. Nock during a run some twelve months after the naming ceremony, when it hauled the 'Midday Scot' from Glasgow to Euston. He expressed particular interest in the ride of the locomotive in order to analyse the effects of the changes made by Ivatt. While the locomotive attained some sustained fast running at 75–80 m.p.h., Nock describes the ride as perfect. On that run the load was no more than 385 tons, and with an allowance of 82 minutes for the section from Carstairs to Carlisle, a distance of $73\frac{1}{2}$ miles, high power outputs were not demanded, but still the water consumption on that run was good. A maximum of 2,550 gallons, or 29 gallons per mile, was a very creditable performance.

A further, much more difficult, run by No. 6256 was recorded by Nock in his book *Sir William Stanier: an Engineering Biography*. The train was the Up 'Red Rose', with a load of sixteen coaches at 560 tons gross on a Saturday running. The train completed two sustained periods of heavy running, the first over the

62.6 miles from Whitmore to the Newbold box in a time of 54½ minutes (an average speed of 68.9 m.p.h.), and the second even faster over the 61.4 miles from Weedon to North Wembley in 52 minutes, an average speed of 70.8 m.p.h. The net time from Crewe to Euston was 151¾ minutes and the aggregate of 124 miles out of 158 were covered in 106½ minutes, an average speed of 70 m.p.h. Details are shown below:

'THE RED ROSE'

NO. 46256 SIR WILLIAM A. STANIER FRS

Distance miles		Time mins	secs	Average speed m.p.h.
0.0	Crewe	0	00	–
10.5	Whitmore	16	31	38.3
24.5	Stafford	28	26	70.7
33.9	Rugeley	37	06	65.3
48.0	Tamworth	48	47	72.3
61.0	Nuneaton	60	15	68.2
73.1	Newbold box	71	03	67.2
		signal check		
75.5	Rugby	arr 76	33	out of course
		dep 77	25	stop
		signal stop		
88.4	Weedon	100	20	
111.4	Bletchley	119	24	72.7
126.4	Tring	133	33	63.8
140.6	Watford Junction	145	10	73.8
149.8	North Wembley	152	17	77.7
		checks		
158.1	Euston	166	42	

As far as can be ascertained, there was no maximum limit ever established for the power outputs on the 'Duchesses', and while it is understood that very high outputs could not be sustained for long periods by a lone fireman, it was possible to mortgage the boiler for a limited time to achieve some exemplary power outputs from the reserves of these great locomotives. This is one of the major advantages of steam over electric or diesel traction, in that with the latter examples, when the controller is pushed to the stops that is the maximum that is available, but with a steam locomotive there are reserves that can be tapped to meet the occasion. This was something the 'Duchesses' were seen to achieve with regularity and outstanding performances were recorded. Most reliable observers would agree that the 'Duchess' class could always produce that extra amount to satisfy the demands of added loadings or sharper timings, footplate crew willing.

With the completion of No. 46257 *City of Salford* and *Sir William A. Stanier FRS*, thirty-eight 'Duchesses' had been built. The gap in the numbering sequence between the 'Princess Royal' class and the 'Duchesses', Nos 6213 to 6219

Sir William A. Stanier FRS, No. 46256, in BR livery, fitted with the final pony truck for these modified 'Duchess' designs.

National Railway Museum, York

inclusive, was never filled. All the class had their numbers increased by 40,000 shortly after nationalization as part of the national numbering scheme, although *City of Salford* was for a short time originally numbered M6257. Completed after nationalization, *City of Salford* was the only new-built 'British Railways' 'Duchess'.

There is some evidence to suggest that the overall weight of the final 'Duchesses' was in fact much heavier than was stated on the design drawings. The axle loadings were correct but overall it has been suggested that they may have been some 10 tons overweight. However, there are no definitive records to support this view, other than purely anecdotal evidence.

The changes on the final 'Duchesses' were the results of the lessons learnt during the Second World War from limited staffing levels and less experienced crews and maintainers. The war also meant higher utilization of traction hauling very heavily loaded trains for longer periods. These two factors were the prime drivers in increasing the mileage between shops and making the accessibility for maintenance that much easier and cheaper to carry out. The knowledge gained was to influence strongly the future Standard steam designs for British Railways.

In addition, consideration was being given to producing detailed figures comparing diesel and steam traction, and with this in mind the LMS built the two diesel electric locomotives 10000 and 10001 at approximately the same time as the new 'Duchesses' were completed. The diesel electric locomotives were designed to produce the same amount of drawbar horsepower as the 'Duchesses' when operated as a pair. The onset of nationalization stopped any plans for comparative trials, however, and although both 10000 and 10001 went into full revenue service sadly no records are available of any comparison between these and the new 'Duchesses' that might have taken place. It would have been interesting to have had some real engineering data with which to make valid judgments on the viability of diesel traction.

Stanier and his team considered a 'Super Duchess' locomotive design and if this had come to fruition, this design could have been the major form of motive power on the West Coast Main Line by the mid-1940s. The basic concept was for an enlarged 'Duchess' based on a 4–6–4 wheel arrangement with a 68 ton eight-wheel tender. The background to the design was the realization that air services between London and Glasgow could become both more convenient, and competitive than the railways. Consequently, acceleration of services to 6 hours or less between the two cities was felt to be essential. Larger trains, normally consisting of at least 600 ton loads were also seen to be necessary. While we have seen that the existing 'Duchesses' were capable of meeting this requirement, the new services would need to be able to achieve this level of performance consistently and under all operating conditions. This would have meant an increase in tractive effort, particularly at the higher speeds envisaged. Typically, 56,000 lb was considered, with a limit on the starting effort achieved making the maximum cutoff 65 per cent, thus giving 42,800 lb.

Clearly this type of output would require massive firing rates which would be beyond the fireman over the length of the journey, particularly as it was thought that a firegrate of 70 sq. ft would be required for this level of output. Consequently, a mechanical stoker was included, hence the trailing bogie design. As the boiler would need to be bigger, the coupled wheel diameters were to be no more than 6 ft 6 in, giving a maximum boiler diameter of 6 ft 10⅜ in, with an increased boiler pressure of 300 lb per sq. in. The locomotive would have been streamlined in the same way as the 'Duchesses', with an overall weight of 119 tons, and an axle loading of 24 tons.

The tender was designed to hold 5,000 gallons of water and 12 tons of coal, although it may have been necessary to consider an even larger tender as mechanical stokers required much smaller coal than was normal on British locomotives. This resulted in some of the finer combustible materials being blown through the tubes and out of the chimney unburnt, an aspect which was not fully understood by British designers at the time. The water consumption on a journey from London to Glasgow has been calculated as 20,000 gallons, again a serious design consideration.

Records indicate that detailed plans were to be drawn up for inclusion in the 1940 Locomotive Programme. Overall general arrangement drawings for the proposed large express locomotive were produced at the LMS wartime headquarters at Watford in December 1942 as part of E.S. Cox's well-argued report, *Post-War Development of Steam Traction Policy*, which recommended that any future passenger locomotive should be equipped with roller bearings, wide fireboxes, thermionic syphons, harder tyres, mechanical stoking and bar frames or cast-steel beds. At the same time a scheme for a large 4–8–4 goods locomotive was proposed with a roughly similar outline as the nonstreamlined

'Duchesses'. It was anticipated that with an availability of 70 per cent for the new express locomotive and the operation of four or five services a day plus some sleeper trains, there would be a need for at least seven and possibly ten, locomotives. If destinations such as Liverpool and Manchester, which the maroon and gold streamliners had served were to be included, it is possible that fifteen 'Super Duchesses' would be required. The records show that in December 1942, the design was considered to be that of a high-speed express locomotive of the future. Typically it was suggested that this locomotive should be capable of taking a 500 ton load from London to Glasgow in 6 hours at an average speed of 67 m.p.h., and achieve an annual mileage of 125,000 miles, with 100,000 miles between service/repair. Clearly, with the social, financial and political changes brought about by the end of the Second World War, the construction of a 'Super Duchess' was no longer a viable option. In any case, major infrastructure modifications would have been needed to allow a locomotive of this size access to the West Coast Main Line. In particular, new larger turntables would have been needed. In addition, platforms, bridges and possibly some tunnels would have had to be modified. None of these changes would have been difficult in engineering terms but they would have met with resistance from conflicting financial priorities at the end of the war. Sadly, no new Stanier designs were produced after the 'Duchesses'.

The modifications to the 'Duchess' design, in particular the changes on the rear truck and cab sides on Nos 6256 and 46257, did not add to the handsome lines of the original design. Nor did the loss of the curved forward section of the running plates on the destreamlined versions, but from an engineering point of view they certainly increased accessibility to the valve gear, and to the firebox and ashpans. These changes show the influence of Ivatt during his time as CME, whose concern was more with the correct engineering solution for the job, at the right price, rather than changes for purely aesthetic reasons. It is probably significant that the modifications he made to the 'Duchesses' were limited to enabling better maintenance as a result of war usage, rather than any fundamental flaw in Stanier's finest locomotive design.

CHAPTER EIGHT

NATIONALIZATION AND EARLY BR SERVICE

Nationalization of the British railway companies was fixed for 1 January 1948 and prior to that great interest was shown in who would be on the British Transport Commission and also the Railway Executive. Overnight the four railway companies were to disappear and the power and influence of the chairman and directors were to go. As with all political reorganizations, the top level of British Railways management was installed more in line with the requirements of the government of the day than of any advantage to the railways and the travelling public.

The Transport Commission was chaired by a senior civil servant and only one of the five members, apart from the former general-secretary of the National Union of Railwaymen, was a representative of the former railway companies. This was Sir William Wood, who had previously been the president of the LMS, and although this was gratifying to that railway, he was largely ineffective, mainly because he was not supported by a headquarters organization following and implementing the decisive ideas of the late Lord Stamp.

The Railway Executive consisted of an influential number of LMS staff, in particular Riddles, who became the member for mechanical and electrical engineering. Also joining the engineering organization were E.S. Cox, E. Pugson and R.C. Bond, all from Derby, with the result that almost all future locomotives would be based on LMS practice. The pride that had existed in the last ten or so years of the LMS was to be carried across to the new British Railways. It was Bond who commented at the time of the inauguration of the diesel-electric locomotives that the initials LMS had been fixed to the body sides in stainless steel characters because 'We did not intend that the origin of the first main-line diesel locomotive built by a British railway company should be easily obliterated or forgotten.'

One of the first actions of the new British Railways was to attempt to gather comparative data using motive power from the four original companies in exchange trials, so that future standard designs could be based on network-wide requirements, a similar problem to that which had faced Stanier when he had first joined the LMS, although it is possible that the designs had been drawn up and

The 'Royal Scot' hauled by No. 46228 *Duchess of Rutland* passes Willesden in 1958.

Rex Conway

manufacturing plans started by this stage. The exchange trials were designed by Riddles and took place in May 1948. No. 46236 *City of Bradford* was designated to compete with a Gresley A4, a Bulleid Pacific and a GWR 'King' class. For the trials on the Southern Region of British Railways, the 'Duchess' was coupled to an ex-War Department 2–8–0 tender complete with LMS lettering on the side, which demonstrated the pride still felt by the original companies.

The performance of the 'Duchess' was disappointing overall, although some occasional peaks of performance were observed. While the general view was that the trials were a sporting contest, the crew of the 'Duchess' believed that the best assessment for their locomotive could be gained by achieving the lowest coal consumption. Consequently, the output performances were well below the capabilities of a 'Duchess'. The locomotive was rarely worked with the regulator more than half opened and only once did she achieve more than 2,000 drawbar horsepower. This was on the climb up Seaton Bank, when a maximum of 2,400 drawbar horsepower was recorded, although this was only transitory, as the figure was well down on the rest of the climb to Honiton tunnel. For all that, *City of Bradford* did produce some of the best ascents of the Western Region gradients to Dainton and Rattery, where she achieved 1,865 and 1,817 drawbar horsepower respectively, and in addition the single time when the regulator was opened fully with 50 per cent cutoff was on the 1 in 42 climb up the WR Hemerdon Bank. To give credit to the reliability of the 'Duchesses', only *City of*

No. 46236 *City of Bradford* at Taunton in 1948 during the exchange trials, still fitted with the sloping smokebox, the original BR number style on the smokebox door and the BR lettering without emblems on the tender. At this time No. 46236 was in LMS black livery. While the quality of this print is less than desirable, the historical content deems it worthy of inclusion.

Rex Conway

Bradford was used for the trial, whereas three individual A4 Pacifics were used over the same period because of maintenance problems. One of these was the famous *Mallard*, which had probably been included more for publicity reasons than anything else. Interestingly, A4 No. 60034 *Lord Faringdon* and Bulleid 'Merchant Navy' No. 21C17 *Belgian Marine* were used on the 'Royal Scot' service and both failed to meet the published timings.

The exchange trials were worked over the routes from Euston to Carlisle, Paddington to Plymouth, Waterloo to Exeter and King's Cross to Leeds. It was during a journey on the latter route that *City of Bradford* nearly came to grief, and the de Glenn leading bogie showed the virtues of its special design. During an Up journey, approaching Peterborough the ex-LMS driver was slow in reducing speed to the 20 m.p.h. restrictions on the entry to the north end curves and traversed them at approaching 60 m.p.h.! That the locomotive survived this treatment is a credit to the original 'Duchess' design, but it does not say much for the cooperation of the ex-LNER conductor driver on the footplate at the time. However, it was reported that the conductor gave advice to the driver but he did not hear it.

The period 1947–8 was a bad time for accidents involving members of the 'Duchess' class, with no fewer than three separate incidents between May 1947 and April 1948.

On 18 May 1947 the 10.00 train from Glasgow to Euston collided with a light engine at Lambrigg box near Grayrigg. The locomotive was No. 46235 *City of Birmingham* and the driver should have stopped at the box to reverse back onto the Down line because the Up line was blocked for repairs. The train passed all the danger signals but luckily no serious results followed this accident, particularly considering the collision happened on Docker Viaduct.

On 21 July 1947 No. 46244 *King George VI* was hauling the 08.30 express from Euston to Liverpool when the locomotive left the track at speed on the section between Atherstone and Polesworth at Grendon. Sadly, five passengers lost their lives in this accident which the inspector's report puts down to badly maintained track, specifically the deterioration of the gauge on the curve. Damage to the locomotive was light, but although No. 46244 was streamlined at the time of the accident, she was shopped for repairs and returned to service as a nonstreamlined member of the class.

The final accident in a disastrous twelve months was the tragedy at Winsford which cost the lives of eighteen people at the time of the accident and a further six later in hospital. Two of Stanier's Pacifics were involved in this serious accident, No. 46251 *City of Nottingham* hauling the southbound west coast postal service, with a load of 625 tons, and No. 46207 *Princess Arthur of Connaught* with the 620 ton 17.40 Glasgow to Euston express. The collision occurred at 00.17 on 17 April 1948, when a young soldier, hoping to shorten his journey home to Windsford, pulled the communication cord and stopped the Glasgow express. The southbound postal train hit the rear of the stopped express after the signalman at Windsford station box had incorrectly allowed the 'Postal' into the section by clearing his block instruments, even though he had not seen the express pass his box. The soldier who was to suffer some of the guilt for this accident later left the armed forces and became a signalman as part of his penance. It has been reported that he more than paid the price for his selfishness and became exceptionally good at his job.

After the war and with nationalization of the railways, the new railway management was trying to deal with a ravaged system suffering from a severe lack of maintenance and investment. At the same time Britain was still trying to build itself up from the stresses and strains of war, deal with the returning servicemen and cope with a government which was pushing through the biggest social changes for many decades. It was against this background that main-line services slowly returned to something approaching normality.

Named trains were reintroduced and new services inaugurated, among which were the 'Midday Royal Scot' from London to Glasgow and the 'Red Rose' from Euston to Liverpool. These services were inevitably 'Duchess'-hauled, and some good performances were given, even though the timings were slower than the equivalent prewar trains. Of particular interest is the 'Midday Scot' service hauled by No. 46242 *City of Glasgow* with a load of 550 tons gross. The train had a point-to-point timing on the Crewe to Carlisle section of 183 minutes for the 141 miles, a fairly easy timing when compared to prewar 'Coronation Scot' services, but this was during the time of great changes on Britain's railways and consequently significant delays could be expected. In any case, No. 46242 achieved some remarkable speeds on this section of the journey, touching 69 m.p.h. at Hartford and Acton Bridge, and accelerating from 64 m.p.h. to 86 m.p.h. on the approach to Lancaster. During the long climb to the top of the Shap the train passed Milnthorpe at 61 m.p.h., with the speed falling gradually to 51 m.p.h. on the 1 in 173 climb to Hincaster Junction. By the time Oxenholme was reached, the speed had dropped to 43 m.p.h. and Lambrigg Crossing was passed at a speed of 35 m.p.h. Overall, the timing was kept between Crewe and Carlisle but numerous signal delays were experienced and the net time achieved was 166 minutes, a gain of 17 minutes on the schedule, and a net average speed of nearly 51 m.p.h.

Another fine performance was the 'Red Rose' hauled by No. 46250 *City of Lichfield*. The Crewe to Euston section of this service was scheduled for 165 minutes over the 158 miles but this was achieved in a net time of 140.25 minutes, with the start-to-stop times being some 2 minutes 41 seconds less than the schedule. This was an overall average speed, including stops, of 58.4 m.p.h. and a net average speed of 70.6 m.p.h. Highlights included 92 m.p.h. between Standon Bridge and Norton Bridge, an acceleration from 43 m.p.h. to 59 m.p.h. on the 1 in 350 gradient to Kilsby Tunnel, an average of 72 m.p.h. on the 15 miles between Bletchley and Tring, and on the latter section the speed never fell below 68 m.p.h.

The driving techniques employed by the various footplate crews on the 'Duchesses' indicated the forgiving nature of these big locomotives and the ease at which they were steamed. Drivers would frequently operate day to day with full regulator, while others would use longer cutoffs and rarely use full regulator, yet in both cases exceptional performances were achieved. Similarly, firemen used different techniques but normally the large firebox was filled prior to the journey start, something which the old Midland drivers would have found very difficult to deal with because of the different firing techniques used on the Midland locomotives. It was probably a good thing that the 'Duchesses' were initially introduced on the old LNWR lines, as the firing techniques matched the ability and skills of ex-LNWR firemen. If they had been on the Midland lines out of St Pancras in the early days it might have been some time before performances came close to those on the West Coast Main Line.

Towards the end of the 1940s the 'Turbomotive', No. 46202, required extensive repairs and for economic reasons it was decided to rebuild it as a conventional locomotive, which emerged from Crewe in August 1952 named *Princess Anne*. While it had originally been conceived as a 'Princess Royal' class

No. 46237 *City of Bristol* on the Up 'Royal Scot' after a diesel failure (steam boiler) and *City of Coventry* on the Edinburgh to Birmingham relief service at Carlisle, 28 December 1963.

John Wickham

locomotive and then built as the 'Turbomotive', in this new form it was of neither class and became for its short life a class of its own. However, it is interesting to note that the change from turbine drive to conventional motion was based very much on the 'Duchesses' and from the front the likeness was very strong. When *Princess Anne* was out-shopped from Crewe it wasn't felt necessary to fit smoke deflectors as with the 'Duchesses', indicating how the different boiler shapes, even with only subtle changes, influenced the flow of smoke and steam along the locomotive sides. The story of No. 46202 has been loosely intertwined with that of the 'Duchesses' and was to do so once more, in a most tragic and dramatic way when, having only run 11,443 miles since leaving Crewe, she was involved in the disaster at Harrow and Wealdstone, and scrapped as being beyond economical repair in 1954.

It was on the morning of 8 October 1952 that the worst peacetime railway accident on British Railways occurred, involving two of Stanier's Pacifics and a 'Jubilee' class. The weather that morning was seasonable, if not exactly foggy. The 07.31 local passenger train from Tring was standing at Harrow and Wealdstone station, at the Up main-line platform, with passengers preparing to board. The train was fully protected in the rear by the coloured light Distant signal set to caution and the outer and inner Home signals set correctly to danger. Without

City of Glasgow, No. 46242, showing the horrific damage sustained after the tragic accident at Harrow and Wealdstone on 8 October 1952. In the same accident the recently rebuilt Pacific, No. 46202 *Princess Anne* was totally destroyed and scrapped. *City of Glasgow* was rebuilt and subsequently re-entered service.

National Railway Museum, York

warning, the 20.15 sleeping car express from Glasgow, hauled by No. 46242 *City of Glasgow*, entered the station at approximately 70 m.p.h. and collided with the rear of the waiting local train. Almost immediately, the 07.55 express from Euston to Liverpool and Manchester, hauled by No. 46202 *Princess Anne* and piloted by 'Jubilee' class No. 45637 *Windward Island*, crashed into the wreckage at approximately 60 m.p.h. The result of this triple impact was absolutely catastrophic, with wreckage strewn all over the tracks and platforms. The degree of damage and the height of the wreckage can be judged by the fact that part of the passenger footbridge across the station was severely damaged in the accident. The death toll totalled 112 people, including the driver and fireman of *City of Glasgow*. With the death of the two footplate crew it was very difficult to find out the reasons why No. 46242 passed all the caution and danger signals without slowing down. The causes of the tragedy will probably never be fully understood, but it is reasonable to suppose that if Automatic Train Control had been available and been used, then the disaster would not have occurred. Both locomotives on the Liverpool express were damaged beyond economical repair and scrapped, but *City of Glasgow* was ultimately repaired and re-entered service with the fully rounded front footplate, similar to the original nonstreamlined members of the class, the only original streamlined member of the class to be so fitted.

The superb performance of No. 6234 *Duchess of Abercorn*, in February 1939 had been considered by many an exception that could only occur either under ideal conditions or as the result of a special one-off effort by the footplate crew. In 1956 full trials were carried out both at the Rugby Testing Station and on controlled road tests between Carlisle and Skipton. The locomotive concerned, No. 46225 *Duchess of Gloucester*, was to prove that the 'Duchesses' could deliver a continuous 40,000 lb of steam per hour, which was an equivalent drawbar horsepower of 2,250. These levels of power and steam production were well outside the continuous firing rates possible for a single fireman. Consequently, to produce these levels of continuous power would need either a second fireman or a mechanical stoker. The fact that these high outputs were exceeded, albeit for short bursts, in regular passenger service, gives some indication of the skills and power of the crews who worked these locomotives. The road testing which was carried out between Carlisle and Skipton produced figures of an indicated horsepower of 2,100 and a drawbar horsepower of 1,570, which was at a firing rate of 3,820 lb per hour.

The greatest continuous steam output from a British locomotive was achieved during the trials when, with a 442 ton load and the Mobile Test Units (MTU), built by the LMS just before nationalization, *Duchess of Gloucester* produced a steaming rate of 38,500 lb per hour. The MTUs were configured so as to increase the load behind the tender to 900 tons, which the locomotive hauled up the 1 in 100 gradient from Settle Junction towards Blea Moor at a steady speed of 30 m.p.h. The tremendous energy that this engine produced was continued for 30 minutes, and although it required supreme effort from the fireman, both steam production and boiler water were kept at a consistent level. The driver on this trial was W. Kelly and the fireman was K. Elliot.

During the latter part of 1944, No. 6244 *King George VI* achieved a run between Oxenholme and Grayrigg stations, a distance of 7.1 miles, in 8 minutes 20 seconds. The loads and timings of this run were compared by the Rugby testing staff with the figures for *Duchess of Gloucester* on the rollers. It was calculated that even with the continuous 40,000 lb of steam generated, No. 46225 would have taken 9 minutes 24 seconds to complete the same journey, over a minute more than the actual results! This comparison gives a good indication of the advantages of steam over other rail traction. When the controller is pushed to the stops on electric or diesel locomotives, that is the maximum. But with *King George VI* the fireman was able to build up the fire to obtain the extra effort and with a full boiler was able to significantly exceed the continuous maximum rates for short periods. The maximum continuous equivalent drawbar horsepower for the 'Duchesses' at 50 m.p.h., based on the Rugby test figures, was 2,260. The crew of No. 6244 achieved a calculated 2,600 on that section of the journey, a very creditable performance indeed. These results were similar to those for *Duchess of Abercorn* in 1939 and were to be repeated in regular passenger service, once again proving the reliability and power of these locomotives.

No. 46257 *City of Salford* with an Up Glasgow to Euston express service near Rugely on 30 June 1953. The seven coaches are a very easy load for the power of the 'Duchesss'. In this view the pony truck differences between the early 'Duchesses' can be clearly seen. Note also that she is still fitted with electric lighting, although not used.

National Railway Museum, York

Interestingly, on 5 September 1957 *King George VI* produced a run comparable to the run of No. 6220 *Coronation* in 1937. No logs of the run are available, reliance being made on the train guard's timing figures, but No. 46244 was hauling the 'Caledonian' express service from Carlisle to Euston when it achieved a net time of 242 minutes (actual start-to-stop time of 253 minutes) for the 299 miles, gaining some 37 minutes on the schedule and averaging 74 m.p.h. for the complete journey. The maximum speeds of 100 m.p.h. were attained near Hindcaster Junction, Castlethorpe, King's Langley and Wembley, while Tring summit was cleared at over 90 m.p.h. This was probably the fastest-ever postwar, long-distance 'Duchess' run.

In 1953 No. 46241 *City of Edinburgh* was used for a special private service for a factory opening in Glasgow, and the service was scheduled for 387 minutes over the 401½ mile journey. On the return run the train stopped at Carlisle for a crew change, and also stopped at Crewe and Watford for passengers; the load consisted of eight coaches at 250 tons. The train was delayed by checks at Plumpton and a 50 m.p.h. speed limit was imposed at Penrith. At Carnforth a maximum speed of 110 m.p.h. was achieved and the Lancaster to Preston section covered in 18 minutes. At Crewe the dining staff requested that things be taken a little easier as the meals could not be served! A more restrained journey ensued and the train arrived at Euston 7 minutes down because of additional delays past Rugby.

City of Coventry, No. 46240, on the turntable at Camdem in 1958. Note that by this time she had been fitted with BR AWS, the battery box, etc., fitted to the running plates, and the protection behind the front coupling.

National Railway Museum, York

A year previous to the trials at Rugby, in 1955, No. 46237 *City of Bristol* was used on the Western Region for dynamometer tests against the GWR 'King' class No. 6013 *King Henry VIII*, which had been fitted with a thirty-two element superheater, a double blastpipe and a double chimney. That Swindon was at last catching up with Stanier's ideas and designs must have been very pleasing for the 'Duchess' designer! As part of the trials No. 46237 was fitted with side-facing lamp brackets.

City of Bristol was set to work the trials trains on both the West of England and Birmingham routes, in particular hauling the 'Cornish Riviera Express', so that both load and route comparisons could be made accurately. This service was booked to take exactly 4 hours for this trip and was a real test both of locomotive and crew, unlike the somewhat easier services of the locomotive exchanges in 1948. In fact, these trials were not an exchange, as *City of Bristol* was lent to the Western Region, was crewed by Western men, and had Western inspectors riding on the footplate. There is a record that No. 46237 also worked the 09.10 service from Paddington to Birkenhead on 27 April 1955.

City of Bristol gave a good account of herself on the 'Cornish Riviera Express' and, while not as consistent as one would have hoped, probably because the Western crews were not as familiar with the driving and firing techniques of the

'Duchesses', particularly considering the differences of the left-hand and right-hand driving positions, No. 46237 was superior at three important points on the route: the very good start away from Reading; on the climb from Westbury to Brewham Summit, when the speed did not drop below 64 m.p.h.; and a minimum speed of 46 m.p.h. at Whiteball. The equivalent speeds of the 'King' were 60 m.p.h. and 37 m.p.h. respectively. The design of the two locomotives gave very similar class 7P efforts but the 'Duchess' was capable of much greater drawbar horsepower. Typically, a comparison of drawbar horsepower between the 'King' and 'Duchess' at a steam rate of 30,000 lb per hour shows the 'King' producing between 75.8 per cent and 93.6 per cent of the 'Duchess's' output at similar speeds.

Speed	Drawbar horsepower	
m.p.h.	'King'	'Duchess'
30	1,640	1,735
50	1,540	1,765
70	1,190	1,570

Clearly, the utilization of steam in the larger-boilered 'Duchesses' was the most significant improvement in design over the 'Kings'. (Further details of this 'Cornish Riviera Express' run can be found in the appendices)

After the impact made by the 'Duchesses' on the Western Region, in early 1956 the 'Kings' were found to have serious problems with their bogies which led to the whole class being withdrawn from service for immediate remedial work. To assist during this period a number of Pacifics from other regions were loaned to the Western, and these included two 'Princess Royals', Nos 46207 *Princess Arthur of Connaught* and 46210 *Lady Patricia*, and two 'Duchesses', Nos 46254 *City of Stoke-on-Trent* and 46257 *City of Salford*. Although the 'Princess Royals' were initially used on the Paddington to Wolverhampton Low Level services, because of the difficulties encountered turning these locomotives quickly enough at Wolverhampton they ultimately joined the 'Duchesses' on the West of England turns. The Pacifics operated the 'Cornish Riviera Express', 'Royal Duchy', 'Torbay Express' and the 'Bristolian' among others out of Paddington. All were based at Old Oak Common shed, with the Pacifics spending just over a month on the services.

No.	Arrived at Old Oak Common	Departed from Old Oak Common
46207	1.2.56	26.2.56
46210	2.2.56	18.2.56
46254	23.1.56	25.2.56
46257	24.1.56	14.2.56

The other Pacifics lent to the Western were nine BR Standard class 5s and four Gresley V2s, the V2s being barred from Wolverhampton (Stafford Road) shed and spending the whole period at Neasden. On 25 and 26 January Paddington was graced with the departure of both 'Duchesses' within 10 minutes of each other, working the 09.00 and 09.10 services as far as Wolverhampton. This invasion of 'foreign' locomotives must have raised some eyebrows among the Great Western aficionados.

During the latter half of the fifties a number of locomotive performance records and logs were produced. The proliferation of such information could be taken to indicate that good performances were more frequent and better than ever before. However, this is unlikely as the quantity of information was more as a result of the social changes occurring during this period. The population was becoming more affluent and thus able to travel greater distances, and annual holidays were now commonplace, and all of this combined with the realization that the life of steam traction really was finite. The advent of main-line diesels and the longer-term discussions on electrification of major routes heightened the realization that steam really was going to be lost for ever. The result was a growing interest in the performance and operation of steam traction all over the country. While this was the beginning of the end for steam, it also produced an Indian summer of interest and appreciation.

A number of 'Duchess' performances were recorded, of which a selection have been included below. The records form part of O.S. Nock's biography of Sir William Stanier. The details of the runs which occurred in the early fifties are shown overleaf and all have the passing speeds at Lancaster and times to Carlisle. The first run shows No. 46221 *Queen Elizabeth* hauling the 'Caledonian', having passed Lancaster 2 minutes late, then a further 5 minutes because of a succession of checks through Carnforth and beyond. Consequently, Oxenholme was passed 7 minutes late but by the time the train had passed Shap Summit all the lost time had been recovered and the train was exactly to time. The summit at Grayrigg was passed at $66\frac{1}{2}$ m.p.h. and the minimum speed on the ascent to Shap was 51 m.p.h. These are amazing speeds involving maximum power outputs of 2,150 and 1,900 estimated drawbar horsepower respectively, albeit for fairly short periods. These outputs have to be compared with the maximum levels achieved on the testing plant of 2,260 edhp. The maximum speed achieved was 92 m.p.h. passing Southwaite.

The figures for No. 46247 *City of Liverpool* are for the 'Royal Scot' service, and although the train was not delayed passing Lancaster, Carnforth was passed at 82 m.p.h. with a supreme effort being made on the ascent to Shap, where the speed was held to 60 m.p.h. over the last $\frac{3}{4}$ mile to Shap Summit, a 1 in 75 incline. This produced a power output of 2,600 edhp, way above the maximum continuous rates of the testing plant – an astonishing achievement.

No. 46241 *City of Edinburgh*, hauling the 'Birmingham Scotsman', was $11\frac{1}{2}$ minutes late passing Lancaster but this was recovered by the time Shap Summit had been reached. The work required to achieve this recovery produced some good power outputs on both Grayrigg and Shap banks, at 1,750 and 1,860 edhp respectively. A maximum speed of 77 m.p.h. was reached passing Tebay.

The final record shows No. 46228 *Duchess of Rutland* hauling a 570 ton gross 'Midday Scot', and while it could not be expected to see high-speed climbing on this service because of the loadings, the power outputs achieved on the ascent to

Grayrigg were good but the outputs on Shap were exceptional. On the final miles to Grayrigg the edhp was 1,640 at 34 m.p.h., but on the ascent to Shap, with Tebay being passed at 64 m.p.h., the average outputs over the 4 miles of 1 in 75 were 2,305, 2,360, 2,065 and 1,800. The climb took 7 minutes 42 seconds and at no time did the boiler pressure drop below 215 lb per sq. in. The footplate crew used real skill and experience to produce these superb outputs, without any appreciable mortgaging of the boiler.

Locomotive		No. 46221 *Queen Elizabeth*			No. 46247 *City of Liverpool*		
Load (tons T/G)		264/280			277/295		
Distance		*Actual*		*Speed*	*Actual*		*Speed*
miles		*mins*	*secs*	*m.p.h.*	*mins*	*secs*	*m.p.h.*
0.0	Lancaster	0	00	20	0	00	72
–			sigs			–	
6.3	Carnforth	7	05	60	4	55	82
–			sig stop			–	
13.6	Milnthorpe	17	32	75	10	48	77
19.1	Oxenholme	22	00	70	15	50	60
26.2	Grayrigg	28	10	66.5	23	17	56/57
32.2	Tebay	32	47	83.5	28	20	77
37.7	Shap Summit	38	05	51	33	15	60
47.0	Clifton	45	52	80	40	37	84
–			–			pws	
51.2	Penrith	49	33	60	45	25	30
61.7	Southwaite	57	31	92	–		83
–			sigs				
69.1	Carlisle	65	42		58	32	

Locomotive		No. 46241 *City of Edinburgh*			No. 46228 *Duchess of Rutland*		
Load (tons T/G)		382/405			524/570		
Distance		*Actual*		*Speed*	*Actual*		*Speed*
miles		*mins*	*secs*	*m.p.h.*	*mins*	*secs*	*m.p.h.*
0.0	Lancaster	0	00	60	0	00	60
–			–			sigs	
6.3	Carnforth	5	38	72	7	05	61
–			sig stop			–	
13.6	Milnthorpe	12	03	76	13	33	68
19.1	Oxenholme	16	57	62	19	35	48
26.2	Grayrigg	24	44	48.5	30	21	34
32.2	Tebay	30	06	77	37	00	64
37.7	Shap Summit	36	28	37	44	37	30
47.0	Clifton	45	35	74	–	–	–
–			–	–		–	–
51.2	Penrith	49	22	–	58	00	–
61.7	Southwaite		pws	15	–		–
69.1	Carlisle	68	53		74	45	

No. 46248 *City of Leeds* passing Willesden during August 1958 with the 'Midday Scot' service. She had only recently returned to service after being repainted in BR red livery.

Rex Conway

Over the next few years the 'Duchesess' were gradually replaced by diesel power on the principal trains, but whenever they deputized there was no deterioration in performance. This was hardly surprising when it is considered that the replacement diesels, the English-Electric Type 4 (ultimately class 40) were capable of 2,000 hp, but giving a maximum drawbar horsepower of 1,350, significantly less than that attained by the 'Duchesses'. Even in the twilight years of these great locomotives, good work was still accomplished in all areas of steam haulage.

CHAPTER NINE

THE FINAL YEARS

Most of the 'Duchesses' were withdrawn from service by the end of September 1964, the last working locomotive, No. 46256 *Sir William A. Stanier FRS*, being withdrawn on 3 October 1964. Whether it was a deliberate policy decision to make this locomotive the last in traffic is difficult to ascertain but in any case it was a nice touch in honour of the great man. Records of this period indicate a number of classic performances from the 'Duchesses', but whether they were really better or more numerous compared to previous times is probably doubtful, as it is believed they are the results of awareness among people of the final passing of steam. Consequently, a greater interest was shown, with a corresponding increase in records, both logs and photographic.

By this time the dieselization of main-line services was in full swing and the 'Duchesses' were increasingly being relegated to the second-rate passenger services and freight workings. Therefore, as a result the locomotives started to become a little scruffy and pride in the class began to fade. In addition, the plans for electrification of the West Coast Main Line were well advanced, so that ultimately the following members of the class were banned from operating under the 25 kV overhead wires south of Crewe.

46225	*Duchess of Gloucester*	46243	*City of Lancaster*
46226	*Duchess of Norfolk*	46245	*City of London*
46237	*City of Bristol*	46250	*City of Lichfield*
46238	*City of Carlisle*	46254	*City of Stoke-on-Trent*
46239	*City of Chester*	46256	*Sir William A. Stanier FRS*
46240	*City of Coventry*	46267	*City of Salford*

This was signified, starting on 1 September 1964, when the remaining nineteen members of the class were painted with a broad diagonal yellow stripe from the top front of the cabside to the bottom rear, broken only by the locomotive number. The restriction was for locomotives over 13 ft 1 in high, No. 46245 being the first to carry the stripe in August 1964, while No. 46256 only carried the yellow stripe for a short time before withdrawal. At the same time locomotive and tender were adorned with the small rectangular high voltage warning plates, to warn crew and maintainers of the dangers of the high-voltage catenary. At the time it was considered that the distance between the highest point on the

No. 46237 *City of Bristol* on a damp 29 August 1964 at Crewe with the 08.05 service from Euston to Holyhead. Note the yellow cabside stripe and the overhead catenary.

John Wickham

'Duchesses' and the overhead cables gave insufficient clearance to meet the high-voltage safety requirements. This is an interesting assessment when compared with the increasing use of preserved steam 'under the wires' today. One little idiosyncrasy in regard to electrical safety was the repositioning of the top headlamp bracket from the top of the smokebox to the middle right of the smokebox door, although not all members of the class were so modified. Photographic evidence shows that No. 46238 *City of Carlisle* certainly had the change in February 1964, as did No. 46241 *City of Edinburgh* in May of that year, but in the same month No. 46237 *City of Bristol* was not modified. This change was also carried out on some of the Stanier 'Black 5s' and 8Fs.

It is understood that in August 1964, just before the identification of the 'Duchesses' with the yellow stripe, a 'Duchess' was waiting at the north end of Crewe station with a Down train when the boiler started to blow off. The jets of steam hit the live wire and the catenary started to move in an initial slow oscillation which reached out to the North Junction. This oscillation increased until it was occurring every 20–30 seconds. The live wire would lift under the jets and then move away out of the steam, fall back again and the process would start again, the amount of movement being approximately 18–24 in. It is also understood that the footplate crew exited the locomotive very, very quickly when informed of the situation by another railwayman.

No. 46256 *Sir William A. Stanier FRS* at Crewe during October 1964. Note the empty tender and removal of the ATC battery box from the running plates. A sad sight, as this was just prior to the locomotive being removed for scrapping. During the last working years, the locomotive was painted with the yellow diagonal stripe.

Rex Conway

After the Harrow and Wealdstone accident, calls were made for the early fitting of automatic train control (ATC), to be known in BR times as the automatic warning system, but it was some considerable time before the majority of main-line express locomotives and track were so equipped. Considering the work carried out on ATC in the late thirties and the experience of the GWR over a very long period, the delay in fitting this important safety equipment is surprising, particularly when accident inspectors had been recommending the installation of some form of train control for a number of years. With hindsight, a number of very serious accidents, including the Harrow disaster, could have been avoided if ATC had been fitted.

The drawings for the ATC system to be fitted to the 'Duchesses' were initially schemed out in 1958, and were finally updated in August 1961, by which time most of the class were either fitted or planned for equipping. Certainly, in June 1962 No. 46249 *City of Sheffield* was so equipped.

The ATC receiver was mounted on the front of the bogie frame, with a protective plate fitted on the rear of the buffer beam behind the coupling links to give protection to the receiver. The most obvious indication of the ATC being fitted was the addition of the battery box and vacuum reservoir cylinder on the right-hand running plate. The battery box was positioned at the point where the cab joins the boiler and was fitted with $32\frac{1}{2}$ amp per hour Nife cells. The ATC indicator was positioned inside the cab on the driver's side.

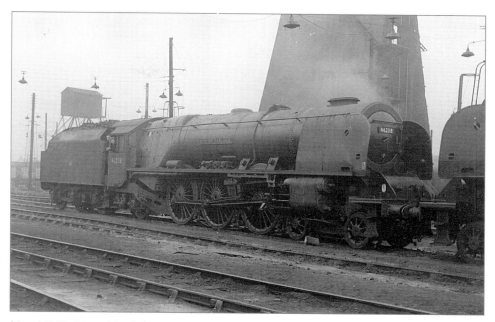

No. 46238 *City of Carlisle* at Willesden Shed on 23 February 1964. At this time her home shed was Carlisle Upperby (12B). Note the ATC battery box and vacuum reservoir on the running plates.

John Wickham

Following the speed recorder changes prior to and during the Second World War, confusion still seemed to reign, as some locomotives were fitted with the Smiths unit in the fifties, typically No. 46256 *Sir William A. Stanier FRS*, even though photographic evidence suggests that this locomotive was not built with this speed recorder. Additionally, the Flaman speed recorder was planned for fitting, and drawings of this device show it to be similar to the original BTH system with brackets and drive like the prewar device, deriving the motion from the rear coupled wheel. Whether any locomotive was ever equipped with the Flaman recorder is difficult to ascertain, but certainly by the sixties the class was fitted with the Smith unit, complete with flexible drive connected to an eccentric coupling above the main coupling rod on the rear driving wheel.

During the sixties, when diesels were being used for more and more top-link services, it was not uncommon for one reason or the other to find that main-line services from Euston started with diesel haulage, but at the change of footplate crews the motive power changed as well, typically to a 'Duchess', at Carlisle or Crewe. It was in these circumstances that disparaging comments were initially made about steam traction, by the incoming footplate crew. In the early days it was not unusual to find that diesel-hauled Euston to Perth trains were failing at a rate of about one in ten, with the result that 'Duchesses' were put on at Crewe or

Carlisle, with the train being already up to 3 hours late. Consequently, the railwaymen had a really difficult task to get anywhere near the timings for the service. Also at this time the top-link crews were becoming younger, with fewer passing through the ranks or stream training, and more concentration being put on the technical requirements of the new motive power, so much so that a 'Jubilee' driver was heard to comment that he had real difficulties in dealing with the cab layout of steam locomotives after being used to diesel traction, even though he had been brought up on steam and was still officially qualified. Another comment regarding the 'Duchesses' was that when under load at slow speeds, the exhaust sounded like the locomotive was taking a breath between beats. Whether this was a compliment or an insult is unclear!

Among some of the comments from the crews of 'Duchesses' in these last years, was that made by the Scottish driver on the sleeper from Glasgow, with a load of over 600 tons gross, hauled by No. 46244 *King George VI*. He was heard to say that he did not understand why Euston station had been demolished when his locomotive could have towed it away! Likewise, No. 46240 *City of Coventry* was on the 'Royal Highlander' service from Euston to Crewe in 1964 when the young fireman on the footplate was heard to say, 'You can keep all your fast cars or motorbikes, give me one of these any day'. During this same trip, while on the ascent of Whitmore Bank, the driver said, 'we will try for 100 m.p.h. on the descent'. In the event the indicated speed on the cab speed recorder was 90 m.p.h., and from the coaches a speed of nearly 88 m.p.h. was recorded. This is still a very creditable run and one that shows the continued loyalty and enthusiasm shown by the crews even when the locomotives were at less than their best.

The main line to Scotland still provided some superb 'Duchess' performances, which was very satisfying considering that it was this route that the locomotive was designed to conquer. In particular, in 1963 No. 46244 *King George VI* showed how it was done. The service was the 'Royal Highlander', which was piloted into Carlisle by a Stanier 'Black 5' and promptly detached. At this point it was realized that No. 46244 was to continue with the train to Crewe. The driver was not over enthusiastic of the prospect of the drive with the 'Duchess' and a heavy load of over 600 tons gross (three coaches plus thirteen sleeping cars, all fully loaded). The train left Carlisle some 17 minutes late, yet in spite of the heavy load made a seemingly effortless climb up to Shap. She was actually noted to accelerate on the short level at Shap station and went on to top the summit of Shap at 38 m.p.h. The speed restrictions on the descent were observed before No. 46244 attained 83 m.p.h. on the approach to Carnforth. The train was checked for signals at Leyland but the summit of Coppul was passed at 44 m.p.h. and finally, after some very good running the train ran into Crewe just 9 minutes late (the net time from Carlisle was 170 minutes). The approaches to Carlisle gave a number of checks caused by the preceding train, the 'Northern Irishman', which was diesel-hauled with a considerably lighter load, and which had left Carlisle some 20 minutes before No. 46244. Both trains were alongside each other at

No. 46229 *Duchess of Hamilton* waits to leave Euston with the 12.55 relief to Glasgow, on 2 August 1964.

John Wickham

Crewe and the driver of *King George VI* was a very much happier man. The log of this spectacular run is shown below.

King George VI was the last of the original red and gold streamlined members of the class, having been completed by 12 July 1940 at a total cost of £10,838 and having originally been named *City of Leeds*. She was renamed in 1941, and thereafter was frequently used on the royal train for obvious reasons. The streamlining was removed in August 1947. At the time of this run she was a Carlisle (Upperby) locomotive, being withdrawn from there during the week ending 12 September 1964.

Locomotive: No. 46244 *King George VI*
                Driver Basford and Fireman Jackson of Crewe North
Train: 21.50 Perth–Euston, 17 August 1963
Load: 16 coaches, 595 tons tare, 620 tons gross

Distance miles		Scheduled mins	Actual mins	secs	Speed m.p.h.
0	Carlisle	0	0	00	–
–	Carlisle No. 13	–	4	15	–
7.30	Southwaite	–	15	27	–
12.95	Plumpton	–	23	41	52
17.85	Penrith	–	29	26	57/60
–	Harrison's Sidings	–	43	53	34/32/35

Distance miles		Scheduled mins	Actual mins	secs	Speed m.p.h.
–	Shap	–	46	57	37/42
31.55	Shap Summit	–	50	10	min. 38
–	Scout Green	–	53	08	64/75
37.00	Tebay	–	55	38	73/76
–	Lowgill Junction	–	59	25	58(60)
42.95	Grayrigg	–	61	18	56(60)
–	Lambrigg Crossing	–	63	21	76(70)
50.00	Oxenholme	–	67	38	78/77/82
–	Hincaster	–	70	21	83/81
–	Milnthorpe	–	71	58	82/80
–	Burton & Holme	–	73	12	72
62.85	Carnforth	–	78	25	63/64
–	Bolton-le-Sands	–	80	20	62
–	Hest Bank	–	81	37	61
–	Morecambe South Junction	–	82	49	58
69.10	Lancaster Central	–	84	51	55(60)
–	Oubeck	–	88	21	58
–	Bay Horse	–	91	08	65
80.60	Garstang	–	96	09	72/73
90.10	Preston	–	106	27	33(30)
–	Leyland	–	115	48	sigs. 8
–	Euxton Junction	–	120	11	30
–	Balshaw Lane	–	122	14	44
–	Standish Junction	–	129	29	–
105.20	Wigan	–	132	52	62/56
–	Bamfurlong Junction	–	134	23	55
–	Golborne Junction	–	139	28	56/57(55)
–	Winwick Junction	–	141	47	–
116.95	Warrington	–	145	34	55(60)
–	Acton Grange Junction	–	147	50	56
–	Norton Crossing	–	150	26	62
124.80	Weaver Junction	–	153	30	63(60)
–	Acton Bridge	–	155	25	65
–	Hartford	–	157	55	66
–	Winsford Junction	–	159	55	70
141.00	Crewe	182	173	50	sigs. on approach

It was during this period that the Beeching knife was rapidly reducing Britain's rail network. It was against this background, combined with the motive power changes which were taking place so insidiously, that the final superb performances of the 'Duchesses' were taking place.

Nationalization had by this time been long forgotten but its effects still produced some interesting results because of the ability to transfer locomotive stock beyond the boundaries of the old Big Four companies and also to a certain extent beyond the boundaries of the BR regions. Consequently, 'Duchesses' were intended to be used on the old Southern Railway routes out of Waterloo. The

No. 46240 *City of Coventry* alongside 'Jubilee' No. 47672 *Anson* at Willesden shed on 26 January 1964.

John Wickham

plan was to take up to twenty 'Duchesses' and use them on the Waterloo to Bournemouth, and beyond services because the existing Southern locomotives were becoming tired. The scheme was finally dropped when the Southern Region civil engineer vetoed the idea because of the significant changes that would have been required, in particular the platform changes at Southampton due to the curves at that station.

There is also anecdotal evidence that No. 46251 *City of Nottingham* operated out of Broad Street station, a schedule which would be extremely unusual as it is understood that the 'Duchesses' were banned from entering Broad Street. More information on this event would be of interest. Another interesting 'away' working was No. 46220 *Coronation* seen in a GWR roundhouse in February 1963, which must have occasioned some strong comment from the resident GWR crews.

As part of any comparison between the 'Duchesses' and Gresley A4s, longevity of the two classes is always used to weight the argument towards one or the other, and as part of that argument is the question of why the 'Duchesses' were replaced with lower-powered diesels, which had a significant failure rate, when the locomotives being replaced had ample power in hand, not to mention life expectancy. In hindsight it is easy to justify the change of motive power, as in purely engineering and financial terms the decision was clear, but at the time the loss of these handsome machines was an act to grieve over. Clearly, that feeling for these engines still exists.

Another creditable 'Duchess' performance was No. 46228 *Duchess of Rutland* hauling the relief 'Midday Scot' from Crewe to Carlisle in 1964. The service left Euston hauled by No. 70054 *Dornoch Firth* at 13.00, and although losing some 4 minutes between London and Rugby, this was fully made up by the time Crewe was reached. *Duchess of Rutland* left Crewe on time, after a 10 minute delay to change locomotives. A dead stand occurred at Weaver Junction for signals, after which a minimum speed of 48 m.p.h. was achieved at Standish. However, after passing Preston at the restricted speed of 20 m.p.h., the 90 miles to Carlisle were covered in $87\frac{1}{2}$ minutes, including the climb to Shap Summit, an average 61.7 m.p.h. start to stop, and a maximum of a shade over 90 m.p.h. attained on the sharp descent from Penrith to Carlisle, where arrival was just 3 minutes late. The log of this run is shown in more detail below. *Duchess of Rutland* was the last of the first four red streamliners, being completed on 17 June 1938 at a cost of £11,302. She was withdrawn during the week ending 12 September 1964 and was based at Upperby at the time of this run. The streamlining was removed during July 1947.

Locomotive: 46228 *Duchess of Rutland*.
            Driver Roberts of Crewe North
Train: 13.00 Euston–Glasgow relief, 26 March 1964
Load: 10 coaches, 304 tons tare, 320 tons gross

Distance *miles*		*Scheduled* *mins*	*Actual* *mins*	*secs*	*Speed* *m.p.h.*
0	Crewe	0	0	00	–
2.85	Coppenhall Junction	–	6	50	–
8.80	Winsford	–	11	13	68
–	Hartford	–	14	56	73/71
–	Acton Bridge	–	17	11	72
16.30	Weaver Junction	–	19	34	sig.
–			24	43	stops
24.15	Warrington	–	34	54	63
–	Golborne Junction	–	44	39	–
–	Bamfurlong Junction	–	47	47	63
35.90	Wigan	–	50	24	50 (50)
39.15	Standish Junction	–	54	39	48
–	Coppull	–	57	32	63
–	Balshaw Lane	–	59	46	76
45.55	Euxton Junction	–	60	50	69
–	Leyland	–	62	05	75
51.00	Preston	–	67	11	(20)
52.35	Oxheys	–	70	04	–
60.50	Garstang	–	78	10	68
–	Bay Horse	–	83	00	72
–	Oubeck	–	85	22	73/70
72.00	Lancaster Central	–	88	06	66 (60)
–	Hest Bank	–	90	46	77
–	Bolton-le-Sands	–	91	46	78
78.25	Carnforth	–	95	29	sigs. 10

No. 46251 *City of Nottingham* shining in the rain at Rugby Midland while working the 05.34 parcels service from Crewe on 5 January 1964. It was not unusual in the latter days of steam to find 'Duchesses' rostered for such services.

John Wickham

Distance miles		Scheduled mins	Actual mins	secs	Speed m.p.h.
–	Burton & Holme	–	100	50	72
–	Milnthorpe	–	102	52	73
–	Hincaster Junction	–	104	41	64/61
91.10	Oxenholme	–	108	16	58
–	Lambrigg Crossing	–	113	48	54/56
–	Grayrigg	–	116	01	63
–	Low Gill Junction	–	117	43	67
104.10	Tebay	–	121	07	76/72
–	Scout Green	–	123	56	55
109.55	Shap Summit	–	127	18	44
–	Shap	–	129	25	74
–	Harrison's Sidings	–	130	45	83
–	Eden Valley Junction	–	135	32	82/83
123.25	Penrith	–	138	19	64 (60)
128.15	Plumpton	–	143	29	89/86
–	Southwaite	–	146	43	81/78
–	Carlisle No. 13	–	151	39	–
141.10	Carlisle	156	154	45	–

By the early sixties the 'Duchesses' were increasingly found rostered on unfitted freight and stopping passenger trains. Typical of these services were the early-morning stopping train from Carlisle to Crewe, which left Carlisle at 06.15. This was normally a very light load, and produced the somewhat incongruous sight of a nearly clean red 'Duchess' hauling such an unimportant service. Similarly a gleaming No. 46251 *City of Nottingham* heading a mixed unfitted freight was a sad duty for a once-proud locomotive. Occasionally even at this late stage these locomotives were rostered to take the express services to London or the North, and typical of this was No. 46241 *City of Edinburgh* hauling a thirteen-coach Perth to Euston express during July 1964, only 2 months before withdrawal. In addition, 'Duchesses' could be seen hauling services such as the 15.45 relief from Carlisle to Euston in April 1963, hauled by No. 46238 *City of Carlisle*, or the 17.35 Euston to Heysham relief hauled by No. 46240 *City of Coventry*.

The latter left Euston without any assistance for the climb up Camden Bank, and after a dead stand at South Hampstead and similar checks in the Tring area, the first 82¼ miles of the journey to a signal stop approaching Rugby were covered in just over 82 minutes, a net time of 78 minutes. Beyond Rugby, *City of Coventry* was impeded by further signal checks, but these were probably because

No. 46254 *City of Stoke-on-Trent* at Willesden shed on 12 April 1963. At this time she was a Crewe North locomotive.

John Wickham

the train was running early. In between the checks the locomotive achieved some solid high-speed runs which are indicative of the enthusiasm to be found among crews of these locomotives even at this late stage. After a near stop at Stafford, the following 24½ miles to Crewe were covered in 26 minutes, including checks on the approach to Crewe. The minimum speed of 70 m.p.h. at Whitmore shows how well these locomotives could perform, and represents a good performance with a 400 ton train.

City of Coventry was completed on 27 March 1940 and was originally built in red livery with streamlining, and cost £10,838 when built. The streamlining was removed in June 1947 and she was withdrawn the week ending 12 September 1964. The final shed for No. 46240 was Willesden, though she had been a Camden locomotive until 1961. A more detailed log of this particular run can be found below.

Locomotive: No. 46240 *City of Coventry*
                 Driver Connolly and Fireman Bowyer of Crewe North
Train: 17.35 Euston–Heysham relief, 24 July 1964
Load: 11 coaches, 374 tons tare, 395 tons gross

Distance miles		Scheduled mins	Actual mins	secs	Speed m.p.h.
0	Euston	–	0	00	–
5.40	Willesden Junction	–	11	34	61
8.05	Wembley Central	–	14	02	64
11.40	Harrow and Wealdstone	–	17	06	65
13.30	Hatch End	–	18	52	66
17.45	Watford Junction	–	22	25	74
20.95	King's Langley	–	25	30	68
24.50	Hemel Hempstead	–	28	35	70 max.
27.95	Berkhamsted	–	31	50	sigs. 53
31.65	Tring	–	36	00	sigs. 55
36.10	Cheddington	–	40	44	sigs. 40
40.20	Leighton Buzzard	–	46	14	62
46.65	Bletchley	–	51	58	74
52.40	Wolverton	–	56	19	82
54.74	Castlethorpe	–	58	08	82/81
59.90	Roade	–	62	38	61 min.
62.85	Blisworth	–	65	27	65/70
69.70	Weedon	–	71	17	76/81
80.30	Hillmorton	–	79	34	76
82.55	Rugby	–	84	58	sigs.
83.20	Rugby No. 7	–	86	38	–
88.10	Brinklow	–	92	31	–
91.40	Shilton	–	96	18	TSR* 20
97.10	Nuneaton	–	104	13	68/sigs. 35
102.30	Atherstone	–	111	36	(70)
106.50	Polesworth	–	115	23	71
110.00	Tamworth	–	118	10	82

* TSR   Temporary Speed Restriction

Distance		Scheduled	Actual		Speed
miles		mins	mins	secs	m.p.h.
116.25	Lichfield	–	122	52	84/sigs. 48
121.00	Armitage	–	127	49	71
124.30	Rugeley	–	130	19	77
127.15	Colwich	–	132	33	79
129.55	Milford	–	134	24	78/sigs. 18
133.55	Stafford	–	140	33	sigs. 8 (60)
136.85	Great Bridgeford	–	144	33	62
138.85	Norton Bridge	–	146	32	64 (70)
143.40	Standon Bridge	–	150	39	67
147.65	Whitmore	–	154	13	70 min.
150.05	Madeley	–	156	17	–
153.25	Betley Rd	–	158	22	–
158.00	Crewe	181	166	24	–

The next superb performance involves No. 46228 *Duchess of Rutland* on the Crewe to London section of the 15.30 Holyhead to Euston boat train. By this time preparations for full electrification were underway when No. 46228 left Crewe some 17½ minutes late, and although the load was average for a 'Duchess', Driver Stoneman probably knew that he had no more than 22 minutes of

No. 46225 *Duchess of Gloucester* running light and returning to Upperby shed after bringing in a parcels service. Behind, No. 46240 *City of Coventry* waits to work the 10.10 relief from Edinburgh to Birmingham. Carlisle, 28 December 1963.

John Wickham

'recovery' time on this easy schedule to Euston. However, what he didn't know was that he would fail to pick up any water at the Castlethorpe troughs, which meant that he had to stop at Bletchley for water. Although 10 minutes had been gained to Bletchley, after the water stop the train was some 17 minutes late. The 46¾ miles to Euston were then run in just under 46 minutes (45 minutes net) which represented a gain of exactly 17 minutes and a punctual arrival. A minimum speed of 58 m.p.h. was achieved over Tring Summit and an overall maximum speed of 80 m.p.h. was achieved – no mean achievement.

Locomotive: No. 46228 *Duchess of Rutland*
Driver Stoneman of Willesden
Train: 15.30 Holyhead–Euston, 8 August 1964
Load: 11 coaches, 335 tons tare, 350 tons gross

Distance miles		Scheduled mins	Actual mins	secs	Speed m.p.h.
0	Crewe	–	0	00	–
4.75	Betley Road	–	8	50	48
7.95	Madeley	11	12	46	51
10.35	Whitmore	–	15	23	63
14.60	Standon Bridge	–	19	02	69/73
19.15	Norton Bridge	22	22	39	75
21.15	Great Bridgeford	–	24	19	75
24.45	Stafford	28	26	01	61 (60)
28.45	Milford	33	30	56	65
30.85	Colwich	35	33	05	69
33.70	Rugeley	38	35	29	73
37.00	Armitage	–	38	03	71
41.75	Lichfield	45	42	13	69/75
48.00	Tamworth	51	46	54	80/76
51.50	Polesworth	–	49	42	75/72
55.70	Atherstone	–	53	20	69/66
60.90	Nuneaton	64	58	15	68/56
69.90	Brinklow	–	67	22	66
75.45	Rugby	85	74	45	sigs. 28 (45)
77.70	Hillmorton	–	78	14	45
82.70	Welton	–	83	45	64
88.30	Weedon	99	88	15	75
95.15	Blisworth	105	93	52	64
98.10	Roade	108	97	25	sigs. 31/49
103.25	Castlethorpe	–	102	06	78
105.60	Wolverton	–	103	51	80/76
111.35	Bletchley	120	109	55	water stop
6.45	Leighton Buzzard	–	8	34	65
10.55	Cheddington	–	12	05	69/67
15.00	Tring	16	16	18	58
18.70	Berkhamsted	–	19	45	69
22.15	Hemel Hempstead	–	22	25	78
25.70	King's Langley	–	25	05	80

Distance miles		Scheduled mins	Actual mins secs		Speed m.p.h.
29.20	Watford Junction	34	27	41	79/76
33.35	Hatch End	–	31	05	75
35.25	Harrow and Wealdstone	–	32	31	80
38.60	Wembley Central	–	35	00	78
41.25	Willesden Junction	50	37	00	TSR 50
43.50	Kilburn High Road	–	40	36	47
46.65	Euston	63	45	50	–

The last sample running log for the 'Duchesses' in their autumn years also involves difficulties with picking up water from troughs, in this case involving No. 46239 *City of Chester* and the troughs near Lichfield. The first 82½ miles from Euston to Rugby were scheduled for 105 minutes, and despite having to slow down significantly for electrification work, No. 46239 arrived at Rugby just over 1 minute early. The departure was 30 seconds late, and there were a number of checks on the way to Stafford, yet *City of Chester* accelerated the train to speeds in excess of 80 m.p.h. between checks. However, she failed to take any water at the troughs near Lichfield so had to stop at Stafford. Due to overhead electrical equipment, No. 46239 had to uncouple from the train while in the middle road and run to the old loco shed to take on water. This involved many reversals and consequently replenishment took 29½ minutes. On return to the train, departure

No. 46249 *City of Sheffield* at Polmadie, its home shed, in December 1962. Under the scruffy exterior is BR green livery!

Rex Conway

was 26 minutes late, but the 24½ miles to Crewe were run in 25½ minutes (25 minutes net) with a fine climb to Whitmore, and arrival at Crewe was only 22½ minutes late.

No. 46239 *City of Chester* was completed on 29 August 1939 in red livery as a streamlined member of the class, and the total cost was £10,838. The streamlining was removed during June 1947 and she was withdrawn during the week ending 12 September 1964. At the time of this run, *City of Chester* was based at Holyhead shed, being the only member of the class at this shed for any extended period, as far as records show.

Locomotive: No. 46239 *City of Chester*
Train: 08.05 Euston–Holyhead, 28 August 1964
Load: 11 coaches, 367 tons tare, 375 tons gross

Distance miles		Scheduled mins	Actual mins	secs	Speed m.p.h.
0	Rugby Midland	0	0	0	–
0.65	Rugby No. 7	–	1	49	–
5.55	Brinklow	–	7	22	62
8.95	Shilton	–	12	58	TSR 26/TSR 25
14.55	Nuneaton	16	22	31	58
19.75	Atherstone	–	27	20	73
23.95	Polesworth	–	30	35	82
27.45	Tamworth	–	33	25	83/sigs. 51
33.70	Lichfield	29	39	22	69/67
38.45	Armitage	35	43	31	77/81
41.75	Rugeley	43	45	49	82/78/80
44.60	Colwich	46	48	00	77
47.00	Milford	48	49	51	77
51.00	Stafford	58	54	51	water stop
3.30	Great Bridgeford	–	5	34	56
5.30	Norton Bridge	7	7	35	64
9.85	Standon Bridge	–	11	30	74
14.10	Whitmore	–	14	53	74
16.50	Madeley	20	16	50	78
19.70	Betley Road	–	19	12	84
24.45	Crewe	29	25	31	–

The 'Duchesses' appeared at London termini only on rare occasions after December 1963, with a few stand-in turns taking place. Prior to that, No. 46245 *City of London* arrived with the Up 'Royal Scot' at Euston on 28 December 1963, and one day later No. 46228 *Duchess of Rutland* came in with a parcels train. The last day on which the 'Caledonian' ran was 4 September 1964, when it was hauled by No. 46238 *City of Carlisle* from Crewe to Carlisle, something that surely must have been prearranged to suit the occasion. Around the same time, the Down 'Midday Scot' to Carlisle was worked by No. 46228, hauling 423 tons and covering the 141 miles in 141½ minutes.

On 21 June 1964 a Locomotive Club of Great Britain special visited Paddington from Shrewsbury hauled by No. 46251 *City of Nottingham*, which resulted in the famous Ivo Peters photograph of the Pacific alongside a GWR 'Castle' at Swindon shed.

The last proper working day for the eighteen remaining members of the class (No. 46226 *Duchess of Norfolk* was laid up in Kingmoor shed with a fractured cylinder, and was condemned along with the rest of the class during the week ending 12 September 1964) was Thursday 10 September 1964, and all but No. 46256 were condemned. There is a possibility that a few may have worked for a few more days beyond this time but this would have been very limited. A week or so earlier, on 29 August 1964, No. 46245 *City of London* was a major attraction at Derby Locomotive Works Open Day, and it seems strange that British Railways should see fit to exhibit a locomotive which within fourteen days would be withdrawn and condemned. This locomotive also held the dubious honour of being the last Stanier Pacific under BR ownership to appear at a London terminus, heading the Ian Allan tour from Paddington to Crewe on 1 September and returning on 12 September 1964.

The last working day by a 'Duchess' while in BR ownership was a Railway Travel and Correspondence Society special, 'The Lowlander', between Crewe and Carlisle and return on Saturday 26 September 1964, hauled by No. 46256 *Sir William A. Stanier FRS*. The load was 416 tons tare, 450 tons gross, and Brook was passed at 74 m.p.h., with minimum speeds of 42 m.p.h. on Grayrigg, 60 m.p.h. at Tebay and 38 m.p.h. over Shap. The locomotive achieved an estimated drawbar horsepower of 2,400 at Tebay. On the Up journey, Shap was cleared in 38¾ minutes. This was the final journey and No. 46256 was taken into store on 28 September, and condemned on 3 October 1964. While it is oft repeated, it has to be asked again to emphasize the loss – why was No. 46256 not put into preservation?

It is very difficult to sum up the life of the 'Duchesses' – they were such a combination of many facets of locomotive design and usage. That they were locomotives with aesthetic appeal goes without saying, particularly in the later years when the streamliners were 'defrocked'. Of course one can argue the pros and cons of the streamlining but at the end of the day the 'Duchesses' were about people, the people who designed and built them, the people who drove and worked them and the people who travelled in the trains they hauled. From the Essex man who was the first traveller to reserve a ticket on the 'Coronation', to the last footplate crews to be rostered on the final journeys, the 'Duchesses' had an impact which was to be long-lasting.

While the 'Duchesses' were considered to be Stanier's finest design, they were also instrumental in bringing the LMS together in something like coherence, and were to nurture a team of engineers and designers who were to have a significant impact on the future of British railways. They were a hard-working class of locomotive which could take all that was thrown at them. I think it is true that by

Euston, and No. 46242 *City of Glasgow* waits to take the Down 'Caledonian' service during 1960.

Rex Conway

and large most enginemen were proud of the 'Duchesses', and even though the firemen considered them to be real brutes at times with their very big, wide fireboxes, the fireboxes were forgiving in their acceptance of the various firing methods. Obviously the coal-pusher helped, but the task was still extremely arduous, particularly over Shap or Beattock. To the drivers the 'Duchesses' delivered a good reserve of power, whatever the requirements, in all but the most adverse conditions, and they handled well regardless of the individual driving technique used. Probably the best accolade for any locomotive is the approval of the footplate crews, and with the 'Duchesses', despite the occasional grumble, the crews were very proud of their locomotives.

CHAPTER TEN

THE PRESERVATION SCENE

Of the thirty-eight members of the 'Duchess' class, only three are preserved and only one of these is still capable of operating main-line steam services. Two notable examples are missing from preservation – Nos 46256 *Sir William A. Stanier FRS* and 46220 *Coronation*. No. 46256 was withdrawn during the week ending 3 October 1964 and No. 46220 during the week ending 20 April 1963. That neither of these fine locomotives survived into preservation is disappointing and could be considered a blunder.

Currently (May 1995), only No. 46229 *Duchess of Hamilton* is operational and she is capable of full main-line steam haulage, but how long this will last is

Alongside the big clock at Paddington station on 4 November 1994, *Duchess of Hamilton* is seen here at platform one. Incidentally, the clock had stopped and was showing the incorrect time!

Author's Collection

No. 46235 at Crewe Works paint shop on 6 March 1966, after being repainted ready to be exhibited at the Birmingham Science Museum.

John Wickham

presently under discussion, as the new director of the National Railway Museum is planning to review this policy when No. 46229 ends her current ten-year certification. This, coupled with the uncertainties caused by the demise of British Rail and the change to Railtrack, plus the approaching privatization of the rail operating companies, makes it a difficult time for steam operators, not least for the 'Duchess'. Circumstances notwithstanding, the opportunities for steam power to continue beyond the new millennium are good, even to the extent that a new Pacific is being built, a Peppercorn A1 to be named *Tornado*. Maybe now that the expertise is being relearnt, a new streamlined 'Duchess' could also be built – they said it wasn't possible with the A1! I would be interested to hear readers' views on this issue and maybe the project could get off the ground.

While uncertainty does exist about the ability to supply 'Duchess' power to the main line, this year (1995) *Duchess of Hamilton* is scheduled to work the 'Cumbrian Mountain Express' over the Settle & Carlisle route and the 'Ynys Mon Express' through to Holyhead, among other main-line passenger services. Steam haulage continues to attract large numbers of enthusiasts, not just for 'Duchess'-hauled trains but all classes of locomotive, and it is hoped that this popularity will help to overcome the difficulties for all steam operators currently being encountered with main-line steam services.

Much has been written about the 'Duchesses' in preservation, so here it should suffice to include brief details of the three locomotives and the current situation regarding each. The three are Nos 46235 *City of Birmingham*, 6233 *Duchess of Sutherland* and 46229 *Duchess of Hamilton*.

NO. 46235 *CITY OF BIRMINGHAM*

City of Birmingham is exhibited in the Birmingham Science Museum, Newhall Street, Birmingham, where it is able to move slowly, back and forth, along 8 ft of track. The track and the locomotive are comprehensively illuminated and all moving parts are shown via mirrors and additional lighting. It was estimated that over a third of a million people saw the locomotive during 1994. Of the three locomotives, No. 46235 is the only one which never steamed after being taken into preservation. It was prepared by British Railways at Crewe over a five-month period, in BR green livery and numbering with the later BR symbol on the tender. No. 46235 never operated in BR red livery. At the time of withdrawal BR also carried out cleaning and other cosmetic work.

The locomotive was subsequently stored in Nuneaton shed between January and December 1965, in preparation for the move to Birmingham. During the storage the locomotive was comprehensively inspected for corrosion and treated with inhibiting chemicals. The locomotive was moved to Birmingham in May 1965 and subsequently the museum extension was built around it. The City of Birmingham owns No. 46235 and there are no long-term plans for any changes in the status of the locomotive, although a bid has been made for lottery funding to carry out improvements to both the locomotive and the site. There is no boiler certificate for the locomotive and it is very doubtful whether she will ever steam again; there are no plans to attempt this.

NO. 6233 *DUCHESS OF SUTHERLAND*

Duchess of Sutherland is presently on static display in the Continental shed at the Bressingham Steam Museum and Gardens, Bressingham, Diss, Norfolk. The locomotive is preserved in the original LMS prewar crimson lake livery, complete with LMS numbering and letters. *Duchess of Sutherland* is shown without smoke deflectors in the original nonstreamlined style fitted with the double chimney similar to *Duchess of Abercorn*, and very handsome she looks too.

Duchess of Sutherland was originally acquired by Butlins for display at the Heads of Ayr Holiday Camp in Scotland. Having been withdrawn for preservation during the week ending 8 February 1964, the engine was moved to Scotland on 21 October 1964 (the tender had arrived two days earlier). Ultimately it was decided that the holiday camp was not a suitable site and the locomotive was moved to Bressingham. It was during that move that No. 6233 was made a Ward of Court! This occurred because of an application from the Lakeside Railways Estates, Carnforth, that the move should be the subject of a postal ballot of the Transport Trust, but on the day set for the hearing in Leeds the application was withdrawn and the locomotive was able to continue the transfer to Bressingham.

Duchess of Sutherland has not steamed for some years at Bressingham and would need some additional work to get her into a position suitable for efficient live steam work, although it is considered that she would take steam. Bressingham

No. 46235 *City of Birmingham* is exhibited in the Birmingham Science Museum, and is seen here in pristine BR green livery during a 'footplate day' when visitors are able to climb aboard. Normally No. 46235 moves slowly along the small section of track shown, and with the aid of special lighting and mirrors all of the motion can be seen working. Note the double chimney and Crewe North shedplate.

Birmingham Museum of Science and Industry

has the facilities for steaming locomotives over a short stretch of track, and No. 6233 was steamed during the mid- to late seventies. Present steaming difficulties have been caused because the firebox tubeplate has cracks in it. While the locomotive was on display at the East Lancashire Railway in 1994 it was surveyed by ELR engineers and their assessment was that the salvage value of the original copper firebox tubeplate would be enough to pay for a replacement steel firebox tubeplate. While this is under active consideration, there are presently no plans to either dispose of or steam *Duchess of Sutherland*.*

* Bressingham sold *Duchess of Sutherland* to the Princess Royal Class Locomotive Trust in November 1995. It is understood that the ultimate intention is to return No. 6233 to main-line steam operation.

No. 6233 *Duchess of Sutherland* showing the side view of the smokebox and the bulbous covers for the steampipes, normally hidden by the smoke deflectors.

Author's Collection

No. 6233 *Duchess of Sutherland* at Bressingham Steam Museum and Gardens in LMS red complete with LMS lettering and numbers. She is shown as built in the original nonstreamlined condition without smoke deflectors.

Author's Collection

NO. 46229 *DUCHESS OF HAMILTON*

Duchess of Hamilton was withdrawn from service during the week ending 15 February 1964, and acquired by Butlins for display at the Minehead Holiday Camp, where she finally arrived in April 1964. However, the holiday camp was not considered suitable for the display of the locomotive and No. 46229 left Minehead on 13 March 1975 to be housed at the National Railway Museum in York. Initially, the locomotive was towed to Swindon for mechanical repairs and repainting, subsequently being moved to York in May 1976. At that time the NRM was leasing the locomotive for ten years from Butlins, but purchased No. 46229 outright at the end of the lease period.

After substantial mechanical work, *Duchess of Hamilton* returned to service on 10 May 1980, on the 'Cumbrian Coast' steam services. Following on from the success of this working, No. 46229 appeared at the 150th Liverpool & Manchester Railway celebrations, following No. 46201 *Princess Elizabeth* in procession, and worked the Liverpool to Manchester Victoria service on 14 September 1980, as well as the Liverpool Lime Street to York via Standedge and Leeds service on 11 November 1980, arriving 20 minutes early at York on easy timings. The Post Office issued a special cover for the occasion. *Duchess of Hamilton* has also been involved on runs between Shrewsbury and Newport which commenced on 31 October 1982. In addition, No. 46229 has been involved with operations over the Settle & Carlisle route, and the 'Shakespeare Limited', which started on 12 May 1985.

To help the operation of steam workings, a turntable was installed at the old motive power depot at Seamer Road, Scarborough, using the old turntable pit. The turntable came from Gateshead and was lengthened and fitted with diesel-electric drive. The facility was tested by No. 46229.

Since *Duchess of Hamilton* has been at the NRM many changes have been made, not least in modifying the tender to increase the water capacity from the original 4,000 gallons to the current 5,000 gallons. This has involved reducing the coal capacity and disconnecting the coal-pusher (this was no longer operational, although still fitted). The work required was too complex in both engineering and financial terms to allow the coal-pusher to operate with the increased capacity water tanks. The additional water capacity was essential to cope with the complete removal of all water troughs on the main line. The water tanks were also found to be paper thin and the opportunity was taken to carry out this repair at the same time as the water capacity changes. The tender of *Duchess of Hamilton*, No. 9802, was originally attached to No. 46239 *City of Chester* from new and was manufactured in 1938. It was coupled to No. 46229 in 1945 and stayed with the locomotive until withdrawal.

During the boiler removal by the NRM it was found that the sloping smokebox front fitted to the streamlined versions of the class was still fitted to No. 46229 but was modified by welding a cover over the sloping bevel so as to make it

The builder's plate fitted to the front of the locomotive. Note also the overhead cables warning plate. Fitted just below the maker's plate is a plate commemorating the 50th anniversary of the *Duchess of Hamilton*, which was unveiled by Sir William Stanier's son, Michael.

Author's Collection

similar in shape to the nonstreamlined type. This is strange as all contemporary records would indicate that the smokeboxes were changed to fully rounded versions, and not modified. The sloping smokebox for No. 46229 was recorded as being replaced in February 1957, and yet in the eighties this modification was found. Subsequent examination of photographs suggests this practice was more widespread than may have been fully appreciated. Comparison of the original nonstreamlined 'Duchesses' and the subsequent 'defrocked' versions would indicate that some had different rivet patterns, and what seems like a separate sheet of smokebox plating appears forward of the chimney. These differences are not obvious on all class members.

A further modification to No. 46229 was carried out without consultation when the cab side plates were renewed and the height of the cornices were raised by 3 in. Presently No. 46229 is preserved in BR red livery, with the BR numbering and tender symbol. The regulator lever from No. 6222 *Queen Mary* is preserved on No. 46229.

Much financial and personal effort has been spent on *Duchess of Hamilton* but the 'Duchess' has given a lot of pleasure to many thousands of people all over the

The tender of *Duchess of Hamilton*, showing the modifications to increase the water capacity to 5,000 gallons, an increase of 1,000 gallons over the original Stanier design.

Author's Collection

country. In addition, there is a great amount of prestige and publicity for the NRM, the operators and the railway companies. Long may No. 46229 run on British main-line steam services.

Perhaps it is fitting that the final words should be those of the late Sir William Stanier. In his acceptance speech after being awarded the Gold Medal by the Institute of Locomotive Engineers, he told the following story:

> I am reminded of a little incident which happened when I was in America in 1936 with the chief civil engineer of the LMS, Mr Wallace. We went to see, on the Pennsylvania railroad, a method which they were using for determining side pressure on rails. We went with the motive power superintendent Frederick Hankins and Mr Duer the electrical engineer. It was one of the electrified sections of the Pennsylvania railroad, and while we were watching the apparatus a number of trains went by hauled by electric locomotives, and nobody took any notice. At last a train came hauled by a K4 Pacific, and everybody stopped to look. I said, 'There you are, Duer, nobody cares a damn for your tin boxes!'

Long may the power of steam and the 'Duchesses' continue.

APPENDICES

APPENDIX 1 DETAILS OF NUMBERS AND NAMES

Number	Name	Name originally selected
46220	*Coronation*	
46221	*Queen Elizabeth*	
46222	*Queen Mary*	
46223	*Princess Alice*	
46224	*Princess Alexandra*	
46225	*Duchess of Gloucester*	
46226	*Duchess of Norfolk*	
46227	*Duchess of Devonshire*	
46228	*Duchess of Rutland*	
46229	*Duchess of Hamilton*	
46230	*Duchess of Buccleuch*	
46231	*Duchess of Atholl*	
46232	*Duchess of Montrose*	
46233	*Duchess of Sutherland*	
46234	*Duchess of Abercorn*	
46235	*City of Birmingham*	
46236	*City of Bradford*	
46237	*City of Bristol*	
46238	*City of Carlisle*	
46239	*City of Chester*	
46240	*City of Coventry*	
46241	*City of Edinburgh*	
46242	*City of Glasgow*	
46243	*City of Lancaster*	
46244	*King George VI* renamed in April 1941 for patriotic reasons (formerly *City of Leeds*)	
46245	*City of London*	*City of Leicester*
46246	*City of Manchester*	*City of Lichfield*
46247	*City of Liverpool*	
46248	*City of Leeds*	*City of London*
46249	*City of Sheffield*	*City of Manchester*
46250	*City of Lichfield*	*City of Nottingham*
46251	*City of Nottingham*	*City of St Albans*
46252	*City of Leicester*	*City of Salford*
46253	*City of St Albans*	*City of Sheffield*
46254	*City of Stoke-on-Trent*	
46255	*City of Hereford*	
46256	*Sir William A. Stanier FRS*	
46257	*City of Salford*	

Note: At the time of nationalization all LMS locomotives were renumbered with the addition of 40,000 to the original LMS number to give the new number shown here.

APPENDIX 2 LIVERIES

Number	As Built	Wartime Black	Experimental Grey	LMS Black	BR Black	BR Blue	BR Green	BR Red
46220	Blue	3/44	–	10/46	–	1/50	8/52	–
46221	Blue	8/44	–	7/46	–	2/50*	1/52	–
46222	Blue	10/44	–	5/46	–	9/50*	12/52	–
46223	Blue	2/44	–	8/46	–	3/50	9/52	–
46224	Blue	10/44	–	7/46	–	5/48†	4/52	–
46225	Red	4/44	–	3/47	–	2/50	2/53	8/58
46226	Red	*/44	–	6/47	11/48	5/49	4/51*	11/58
46227	Red	1/44	–	3/47	–	5/48†	5/53	–
46228	Red	4/44	–	11/47	–	8/50	8/55	6/58
46229	Red	8/43*	–	12/47	–	1/50*	3/52	9/58
46230	Red	–	–	9/46	–	5/48†	3/52	–
46231	Red	8/45*	–	9/46	–	5/48†	11/53	–
46232	Red	2/45	–	9/47	–	–	11/51*	–
46233	Red	–	–	9/46	–	–	12/52*	–
46234	Red	–	3/46	–	–	5/48†	1/52	–
46235	Red	3/43	–	4/46	–	10/50*	4/53	–
46236	Red	4/44	–	12/47	–	–	8/55	7/58
46237	Red	8/43*	–	2/47	–	8/49*	8/52*	–
46238	Red	*/43	–	8/46	3/49	–	10/53	6/58
46239	Red	3/44*	–	9/47	–	6/50*	7/54*	–
46240	Red	11/45	–	7/47	–	1/50	9/54*	7/58
46241	Red	5/43*	–	2/47	–	5/48†	4/53*	–
46242	Red	5/44	–	5/47	–	8/49	11/53	–
46243	Red	1/44	–	–	–	6/49	1/54*	10/58
46244	Red	New	–	8/47	–	9/48†	5/53	10/58
46245	Black	New	–	11/47	–	–	4/53	12/57
46246	Black	New	–	11/46	11/48	–	5/53*	10/58
46247	Black	New	–	2/47	–	–	1/54*	5/58
46248	Black	New	–	1/47	3/49	–	8/53*	6/58
46249	Black	New	–	11/46	–	8/50*	1/53*	–
46250	Black	New	–	7/47	–	3/50*	9/52*	–
46251	Black	New	–	6/47	4/49	–	10/51*	11/58
46252	Black	New	–	11/48*	3/49	*/50	1/54*	–
46253	Black	–	–	New	–	–	10/53*	–
46254	Black	–	–	New	–	8/50*	1/53*	9/58
46255	Black	–	–	New	–	6/50	4/53	–
46256	Black	–	–	New	11/48	3/51*	5/54*	5/58
46257	Black	–	–	–	New	*	11/52*	–

Notes: * Possible that locomotive went into service a month or two later or in some cases month not known.

† Experimental blue livery applied at first painting prior to BR Blue.

Nos 46237/56/57 ran with tenders marked 'BRITISH RAILWAYS'.

APPENDIX 3 DATES OF SIGNIFICANT CHANGES

Number	Date new	Streamlining removed	Date smoke deflectors fitted	Date of BR number	Date withdrawn
Single chimney when built, streamlined					
46220	6/37	9/46	9/46	7/48	4/63
46221	6/37	5/46	5/46	10/48	5/63
46222	6/37	5/46	5/46	9/48	10/63
46223	7/37	8/46	8/46	3/49	10/63
46224	7/37	5/46	5/46	5/48	10/63
46225	5/38	2/47	2/47	6/48	9/64
46226	5/38	6/47	6/47	9/48	9/64
46227	6/38	2/47	2/47	5/48	12/62
46228	6/38	7/47	7/47	7/48	9/64
46229	9/38	11/47	11/47	7/48	2/64 P
Single chimney when built, nonstreamlined					
46230	6/38	–	9/46	5/48	11/63
46231	6/38	–	9/46	5/48	12/62
46232	7/38	–	2/45	5/48	12/62
46233	7/38	–	9/46	10/48	2/64 P
46234	8/38	–	3/46	10/48	1/63
Double chimney when built, streamlined					
46235	7/39	4/46	4/46	5/48	9/64 P
46236	7/39	12/47	12/47	4/48	3/64
46237	8/39	1/47	1/47	7/48	9/64
46238	9/39	11/46	11/46	3/49	9/64
46239	9/39	6/47	6/47	8/48	9/64
46240	3/40	6/47	6/47	6/48	9/64
46241	4/40	1/47	1/47	5/48	9/64
46242	5/40	3/47	3/47	5/48	10/63
46243	6/40	5/49	5/49	4/48	9/64
46244	7/40	8/47	8/47	8/48	9/64
46245	6/43	8/47	8/47	8/48	9/64
46246	8/43	9/46	9/46	11/48	1/63
46247	9/43	5/47	5/47	11/48	5/63
46248	10/43	12/46	12/46	3/49	9/64
Double chimney when built, nonstreamlined					
46249	4/44	–	11/46	4/48	11/63
46250	5/44	–	3/46	2/49	9/64
46251	6/44	–	8/46	5/48	9/64
46252	6/44	–	3/45	4/49	5/63
46253	9/46	–	New	9/49	5/63
46254	9/46	–	New	7/49	9/64
46255	10/46	–	New	6/49	9/64
46256	12/47	–	New	5/48	10/64
46257	2/48*	–	New	5/48	9/64

Notes: P Preserved
        * Not released to traffic until 5/48.

APPENDIX 4 CHIMNEY AND SMOKEBOX CHANGES

Number	Date of double chimney	Date smokebox changed
46220	12/44	2/57
46221	11/40	9/52
46222	8/43	8/53
46223	11/41	8/55
46224	5/40	10/54
46225	6/43	1/55
46226	7/42	11/55
46227	12/40	5/53
46228	9/40	1/57
46229	4/43	2/57
46230	10/40	–
46231	6/40	–
46232	1/43	–
46233	3/41	–
46234	2/39	–
46235	New	7/52
46236	New	11/53
46237	New	5/56
46238	New	10/53
46239	New	2/57
46240	New	5/57
46241	New	2/58
46242	New	11/53
46243	New	11/58
46244	New	7/53
46245	New	12/57
46246	New	5/60
46247	New	5/58
46248	New	6/58
46249	New	–
46250	New	–
46251	New	–
46252	New	–
46253	New	–
46254	New	–
46255	New	–
46256	New	–
46257	New	–

APPENDIX 5 DETAILED COSTS

Number	LMS workshop order No.	Lot No.	Estimated cost (£)*	Completed cost (£)†	Tender cost (£)
46220 46221 46222 46223 46224	402	138	10,400	11,813	1,556
46225 46226 46227 46228 46229	408	145	13,800	10,136	1,601
46230 46231 46232 46233 46234	408	145	13,800	9,585	1,509
46235 46236 46237 46238 46239 46240 46241 46242 46243 46244	414	150	12,150	9,437	1,549
46245 46246 46247 46248	415 " " "	150 " " "	12,150 " " "	9,324 10,182 9,037 9,445	1,670 " " "
46249 46250 46251 46252	415	150	12,150	10,069	1,670
46253 46254 46255	464	184	15,170	15,460	‡
46256 46257	464	184	15,170	18,248	3,163

Notes: * Estimate costs are costs for each locomotive *including* tender.
 † Costs are average across the batch per individual locomotive.
 ‡ Costs not quoted for tender but believed to be £3,163.

APPENDIX 6 MILEAGES

Number	Average annual mileage	Total lifetime mileage
46220	58,741	1,527,266
46221	58,162	1,512,212
46222	55,723	1,448,790
46223	56,222	1,461,772
46224	56,091	1,402,275
46225	66,183	1,742,642*
46226	67,764	1,423,044
46227	57,658	1,210,818
46228	68,002	1,428,042
46229	67,241	1,412,061†
46230	59,764	1,255,044
46231	60,100	1,262,100
46232	57,998	1,217,958
46233	67,113	1,409,373
46234	69,678	1,463,238
46235	63,946	1,278,920
46236	66,642	1,332,840
46237	72,437	1,448,740
46238	65,951	1,319,020
46239	76,256	1,525,120
46240	70,949	1,348,031
46241	72,202	1,371,838
46242	68,818	1,307,542
46243	64,810	1,231,390
46244	71,495	1,358,405
46245	68,968	1,103,488
46246	71,256	1,140,096
46247	70,574	1,129,184
46248	69,944	1,119,104
46249	69,857	1,047,855
46250	69,057	1,035,855
46251	63,250	948,750
46252	65,065	975,975
46253	70,107	911,391
46254	63,760	828,880
46255	63,398	824,174
46256	63,504	762,048
46257	69,548	765,028

Notes: * Highest mileage of the class.
       † Not including mileage in the USA.
All mileage is calculated up to 1959 as records beyond this time are incomplete for a proportion of the class.

Interestingly, locomotives based at Polmadie ran fewer miles than others. It is not believed that this is indicative of poorer availability compared to the locomotives based south of the border, but of the frequent relatively short journeys that the Scottish locomotives carried out.

APPENDIX 7 BOILER DETAILS

Number	First boiler		Last boiler	No. of changes
46220	9937		10296	7
46221	9938		10298	7
46222	9939		10289	8
46223	9940		10299	9
46224	9941		10288	11
46225	10297		10693	9
46226	10298		10640	9
46227	10299		9938	8
46228	10300		10291	8
46229	10306		10297	8
46230	10301		10694	8
46231	10302		10646	8
46232	10303		10303	8
46233	10304		10641	8
46234	10305		12470	7
46235	10287		9940	8
46236	10288		10301	7
46237	10289		10645	7
46238	10290		10287	7
46239	10291		10306	7
46240	10292		9941	7
46241	10293		10643	6
46242	10294		10639	6
46243	10295		10290	8
46244	10296		10644	7
46245	9940	(second-hand)	10292	4
46246	10645		9937	6
46247	10303	(second-hand)	12472	5
46248	10638	(second-hand)	10294	6
46249	10644		9939	6
46250	10646		10300	5
46251	10693		10295	5
46252	10694		10304	6
46253	12470		13043	5
46254	12471		10642	5
46255	12472		10305	4
46256	12473		13044	4
46257	12474		12474	3

The 'Duchess' class had forty-four boilers built for the thirty-eight locomotives and all were interchangeable. These changes normally took place during heavy general repairs. Most of the class entered service with brand-new boilers but, as shown above, three were fitted with second-hand boilers which had previously been overhauled and were originally built for earlier members of the class.

Boilers Nos 13043 and 13044 were built for stock in 1949–50.

APPENDIX 8 PRINCIPAL SHED ALLOCATIONS

Number	Camden	Crewe N.	Polmadie	Carlisle Upperby	Edge Hill	Holyhead
	1B	5A	27A/66A	12B/12A/12B	8A	7C/6J
46220	1937	9/58	12/39	1960		
46221	1937	7/58				
	6/59	10/60		4/62		
46222	1937		12/39 till withdrawal			
46223	1937		12/39 till withdrawal			
46224	1937		12/39 till withdrawal			
46225	1938	1940				1939
	1943	1946				
	1947	1949				
	1955			1959		
46226	1938	1940				1939
	1943					1946
46227	1938	1940				1939
	1943	1947	1948	1946		
46228	1938	1940		1946		10/39
	1943	1957		1959		
46229		1938				
	1943	1942	USA 1939–42			
	1948	1947				
	1952	1949				
		1960			Last	
46230	1938		1940 till withdrawal			
46231	1938		1940 till withdrawal			
46232	1938		1940 till withdrawal			
46233	1938	1944			1960	
46234	1938	1943				
	1959			1959		
46235	1939	1944 till withdrawal				
46236	1939	1944				
	1951			1958		
46237	1939			1958		
46238	1939	1939		1947		
46239	1939					1963*
46240	1940 till withdrawal (Willesden 1A after 1961)					
46241	1940	1958			Last	
46242	1940		1944			
	1948	1953				
	1954		1961			
46243	1940	1948			1948	
	1960†	1958		1958	Last	
46244	1940			1958		
46245	1943 till withdrawal (Willesden 1A after 1961)					
46246	1943	1948				
	1960 (Willesden 1A after 1961)					
46247	1943 till withdrawal (Willesden 1A after 1961)					
46248	1943	1948				
46249	1944			1948		
	1954	1958	Last			
46250		1944	1944	1946		
	1949			1958		

Notes: * Previously at Willesden 1A from 1961.
         † Then to Willesden from 1961.

Number	Camden	Crewe N.	Polmadie	Carlisle Upperby	Edge Hill	Holyhead
	1B	5A	27A/66A	12B/12A/12B	8A	7C/6J
46251		1944	1944	1946		
	1948	1948				1948
	1949			1949		
	1950			1950		
		1956				
		1957		1957		
46252		1944				
	1950 to 1962*	1952 alternating		1960		
46253	1946			1949		
	1952	1957				
46254	1946	1952		1949		
	1953	1957		1953		
46255	1946			1948		
		1952		1953		
46256	1948	1948		1959		
	1960	1960				
46257	1948			1959		

Notes: * To Willesden from 1961.

APPENDIX 9 TENDER CHANGES

Number	Tenders
46220	9703–new, 9803–1944, 9703–1944, 9804–1946, 9705–1949
46221	9704–new, 9816–1961, 9359–1962, (ex-'Princess Royal' type – no coal-pusher)
46222	9705–new, 9804–1949
46223	9706–new, 9748–1946
46224	9707–new, 9748–1945, 9706–1946*
46225	9743–new, 9749–1945, 9799–1949
46226	9744 throughout
46227	9745 throughout
46228	9746 throughout
46229	9747–new, 9802–1945 (now modified for preserved steam running)
46230	9748–new, 9707–1945
46231	9749–new, 9812–1945
46232	9750 throughout
46233	9751 throughout
46234	9752 throughout
46235	9798 throughout
46236	9799–new, 9749–1949, 9807–1952 (fitted with eight-wheel Austerity tender during exchange trials)
46237	9800–new, 9804–1944, 9800–1944
46238	9801 throughout
46239	9802–new, 9749–1945
46240	9803–new, 9703–1944, 9803–1944
46241	9804–new, 9805–1944, 9811–1953, 9703–1956, 9811–1956
46242	9805–new, 9703–1946, 9816–1951, 9703–1951, 9811–1956, 9703–1956
46243	9806 throughout
46244	9807–new, 9808–1945
46245	9808–new, 9807–1945, 9811–1952, 9805–1953
46246	9809–new, 9749–1961
46247	9810–new, 9811–1944, 9807–1952, 9749–1952, 9808–1961
46248	9811–new, 9810–1944
46249	9812 – new, 9747–1945
46250	9813 throughout
46251	9814 throughout
46252	9815 throughout
46253	9816–new, 9703–1951, 9816–1951, 9750–1954, 9816–1955, 9704–1961
46254	9817 throughout
46255	10622 throughout
46256	10623 throughout
46257	10624 throughout

Notes: * Fitted with nonstreamlined tender ex-No. 46230 then refitted with tender belonging to No. 46223 when *Princess Alice* was also fitted with a nonstreamlined tender.

APPENDIX 10 DATES OF CITY NAMING CEREMONIES

Number	Name	Date
46235	*City of Birmingham*	20 March 1945
46240	*City of Coventry*	6 November 1945
46245	*City of London*	20 July 1943
46246	*City of Manchester*	3 September 1943
46248	*City of Leeds*	2 December 1943
46249	*City of Sheffield*	1 November 1944
46250	*City of Lichfield*	20 June 1944
46251	*City of Nottingham*	4 October 1945
46252	*City of Leicester*	9 October 1944
46254	*City of Stoke-on-Trent*	20 September 1946
46257	*City of Salford*	3 June 1948

Apart from No. 46248, which was named at Euston, all the above visited the city honoured for the naming ceremony. Nos 46235/40/54 had the city arms fitted above the name-plate.

APPENDIX 11 'CORNISH RIVIERA EXPRESS', PADDINGTON TO NEWTON ABBOT, 1956

LOG DETAILS

Locomotive: No. 46237 *City of Bristol*

Load:			
To Heywood Road	460 tons tare	490 tons gross	
To Exeter	393 tons tare	420 tons gross	

Distance miles		Scheduled mins	Actual mins secs	Speed m.p.h.
0.0	Paddington	0	0 00	–
5.7	Ealing Broadway		8 58	58
9.1	Southall	12.5	12 17	65
13.2	West Drayton		15 49	73
18.5	Slough	21.0	20 02	76
24.2	Maidenhead	26.0	24 39	72
36.0	Reading	37.0	35 23	–
—			pws	–
44.8	Aldermaston		47 42	56
53.1	Newbury	55.0	56 18	62
58.5	Kintbury		61 13	70
66.4	Bedwyn	68.0	68 38	57/65
70.1	Savernake	72.5	72 19	54
75.3	Pewsey		76 53	78
81.1	Patney	82.5	81 23	75
86.9	Lavington		85 43	83
94.6	Heywood Road Junction	93.0	91 34	75
100.3	Clink Road Junction		96 28	61
102.3	Blatchbridge Junction	100.5	98 15	71.5
108.3	Brewham Box		103 27	64
			–	77
115.1	Castle Cary	113.5	108 57	slack
130.8	Curry Rivel Junction		122 20	82.5
—			pws 15	
138.0	Cogload Junction		130 34	69
142.7	Taunton	136.5	134 49	66
149.8	Wellington		141 25	62/64
152.6	Milepost 173		145 38	48
153.6	Whiteball Box	149.0	146 45	46
158.6	Tiverton Junction		149 52	85
165.1	Hele		155 04	72
170.0	Stoke Canon		159 02	75.5
173.5	Exeter	167.5	162 23	slack
178.3	Exminster		167 21	64
185.7	Dawlish		176 13	slack
188.5	Teignmouth		180 05	50 max.
193.7	Newton Abbot	192.0	187 21	–

BIBLIOGRAPHY

Allan, C.J., *British Pacific Locomotives*, Ian Allan, 1962.
Bellwood, J. and Jenkinson, D., *Gresley and Stanier, A Centenary Tribute*, National Railway Museum, 1976.
Bushell, G., *Willesden Footplate Memories*, Bradford Barton, 1982.
Cox, E.S., *Post-War Development of Steam Traction*, LMS paper, National Railway Museum, 23 December 1942.
Evans, M., *Pacific Steam*, Percival Marshall, 1961.
Griffiths, D., *Locomotive Engineers of the LMS and its Major Constituent Companies*, Patrick Stephens Ltd, 1991.
Haresnape, G., *Stanier Locomotives, A Pictorial History*, Ian Allan, 1981.
Hughes, G., *LNER 4–6–0s at Work*, Ian Allan, 1988.
Jenkinson, D., *Profile of the Duchesses*, Oxford Publishing Company, 1982.
Johansen/LMS, *Streamlining Experiments on 4–6–2 Locomotive No. 6220 Coronation*, memo J,12/37, National Railway Museum, 24 September 1937.
Langridge, E.A., *The Design and Construction of the LMS Duchess Class*, draft paper, National Railway Museum, undated.
McKenna, F., *The Railway Workers 1840–1970*, Faber and Faber Ltd, 1980.
Mullay, A.J., *Streamlined Steam*, David & Charles, 1994.
Nock, O.S., *A History of the LMS*, George Allen & Unwin.
    Part 1, The First Years, 1923–1930, third impression, 1988.
    Part 2, The Record Breaking Thirties, 1931–39, third impression, 1988.
    Part 3, The War Years and Nationalisation, 1939–48, third impression, 1988.
——, *Sir William Stanier: an Engineering Biography*, Ian Allan, 1964.
Oldham, K., *Steam in Wartime Britain*, Alan Sutton Publishing Ltd, 1993.
Reed, J.B., *Crewe Locomotive Works and its Men*, David & Charles, 1982.
Rowledge, J.W.R., *Engines of the LMS built 1923–51*, Oxford Publishing Company, 1975.
——, *The LMS Pacifics*, Locomotive Monograph Series, David & Charles, 1987.
Thomas St John, D. and Whitehouse, P., *The Great Days of Express Trains*, David & Charles, reprinted 1993.
——, *The Trains We Loved*, David & Charles, 1994.
Williams, C., Min/3 Purchase, National Railway Museum, 1938 to 1942.
—— Min/4 Purchase, National Railway Museum, 1938 to 1942.

BR AWS General Arrangement, D58-23519, National Railway Museum.
Flaman Speed Recorder D59-24436, National Railway Museum.
LMS Technical Box, National Railway Museum.
Steam Railway Nos 175–178, EMAP Apex Publications, 1994.
Steam World Nos 79–92, EMAP Apex Publications, 1994.

INDEX